"If you want a theology book packed full of footnotes and words Webster doesn't know, then this book is *not* for you. English makes the Christian tradition sing! *Theology Remixed* is a robust and accessible invitation to a thoughtful and living faith. It not only offers a refreshing vision of theology but repeatedly works every abstract idea down to the daily life of a disciple. English remixes theology beyond the old battle lines by offering a more beautiful and compelling alternative. This is a book too good to miss!"

Tripp Fuller, host of the *Homebrewed Christianity* podcast, Ph.D. student at Claremont Graduate University and minister of youth at Neighborhood Church of Palos Verdes, California

"Adam English mixes it up in this engaging treatment of Christianity, drawing deeply from church history and tradition to explore theology's useful analogues in story, game, language and culture. *Theology Remixed* blends careful scholarship with insights from popular culture and personal experience to craft a compelling vision of the Christian faith as God's good news for the world in our time and every time."

Debra Dean Murphy, assistant professor of religion, West Virginia Wesleyan College, and author of *Teaching That Transforms: Worship as the Heart of Christian Education*

"*Theology Remixed* is an attempt, and a successful one, to imagine new paths that lead us to very ancient truths. By expanding the analogies of language, story, game and culture, English shows us how Christians today might participate more fully in what God is doing in the world. His combination of rigorous scholarship and profoundly practical wisdom makes this an accessible, thought-provoking work. This is an excellent introduction to, and an example of, how to do theology."

Elizabeth Newman, professor of theology and ethics, Baptist Theological Seminary at Richmond

"This is a good work! I found myself saying 'Amen!' repeatedly as I read through the text. In a cultural moment marked by the white heat of the polemical new atheism, English offers a most appropriate response: a passionate, discursive witness to the truth of the gospel of Jesus Christ. In so doing, he bears witness to what Stanley Hauerwas has called an essential task of ministry: to teach the language called Christian so as to speak Christian rightly. Reading Scripture and tradition with charity and cherishing its wisdom, English wonderfully employs a pedagogical strategy of using four analogies (story, game, language, culture) to offer an invigorating and faithful understanding of Christian faith and life. His discussion of Christianity as game is inventive and most illuminating for a culture obsessed with sports and gaming; the discussion of Christianity as language is worth the price of admission. Written in an accessible style, this timely book is a small catechism of the Christian faith which can guide preachers and teachers, in the service of the triune God, to help those they serve know how to speak Christian."

Mark S. Medley, associate professor of theology, Baptist Seminary of Kentucky

"*Theology Remixed* by Adam English is a timely book, (re)introducing classic Christian thought to many readers who might otherwise be unfamiliar with it. And, for those like me who revel in the rich treasury of Christian theology, it's like a rewarding conversation with old friends."

Tony Jones, theologian-in-residence, Solomon's Porch, and author of *The Teaching of the Twelve: Believing & Practicing the Primitive Christianity of the Ancient Didache Community* (http://tonyj.net)

"The church today exists in an often bewildering situation: attacked from without and dispirited within. In a time when the normal patterns of thinking about the faith ring hollow for many, Adam English offers the church ways of recovering the deep wisdom of the Christian tradition. He does so with a helpful mixture of astute theology, pastoral sensitivity and an unfailingly irenic spirit. Wearing his erudition lightly, English proves himself a trustworthy guide through a range of large and perplexing ideas and issues. Along the way, he models the wisdom of the faith he commends."

Philip E. Thompson, Sioux Falls Seminary, South Dakota

ADAM C. ENGLISH

THEOLOGY

R E M I X E D

Christianity as Story, Game,
Language, Culture

IVP Academic

An imprint of InterVarsity Press
Downers Grove, Illinois

InterVarsity Press
P.O. Box 1400, Downers Grove, IL 60515-1426
World Wide Web: www.ivpress.com
E-mail: email@ivpress.com

InterVarsity Press® is the book-publishing division of InterVarsity Christian Fellowship/USA®, a movement of students and faculty active on campus at hundreds of universities, colleges and schools of nursing in the United States of America, and a member movement of the International Fellowship of Evangelical Students. For information about local and regional activities, write Public Relations Dept., InterVarsity Christian Fellowship/USA, 6400 Schroeder Rd., P.O. Box 7895, Madison, WI 53707-7895, or visit the IVCF website at <www.intervarsity.org>.

Design: Cindy Kiple
Images: Oscar Vargas/Getty Images

ISBN 978-0-8308-3874-5

Printed in the United States of America ∞

Library of Congress Cataloging-in-Publication Data

English, Adam C., 1974-
  Theology remixed: Christianity as story, game, language, culture/
Adam C. English.
    p. cm.
  Includes bibliographical references and index.
  ISBN 978-0-8308-3874-5 (pbk.: alk. paper)
  1. Philosophical theology. 2. Christianity—Philosophy. I. Title.
  BT40.E64 2010
  230.01—dc22

2010019872

P	19	18	17	16	15	14	13	12	11	10	9	8	7	6	5	4	3	2	1
Y	26	25	24	23	22	21	20	19	18	17	16	15	14	13	12	11	10		

To my parents

CONTENTS

PART 4: CHRISTIANITY AS CULTURE

PREFACE

I PICKED UP THE RINGING PHONE IN MY OFFICE.[1] It was a friend from Quail Ridge Books of Raleigh asking if I would be interested in debating a certain Christopher Hitchens who would be coming to the store on his book publicity tour in about two months. Hitchens, the nationally recognized columnist and commentator, would be releasing a new book, *God Is Not Great: How Religion Poisons Everything*. I accepted the invitation, thinking it would be an intimate conversation in a quiet bookstore. As the date approached, the event began to mushroom into a much larger affair than anyone had anticipated. Hitchens had been making appearances on late night shows, radio programs, magazines and local papers. The bookstore moved the debate to the Unitarian Universalist Fellowship of Raleigh, but even it did not provide sufficient space for the droves of people that showed up.

Ushers began turning people away thirty minutes prior to the event because the auditorium was filled to capacity, with over five hundred people packed against the walls and everywhere else. They were not coming to see me of course, an inexperienced and unknown assistant professor of theology from Campbell University, but the flashy and articulate atheist Hitchens, who at the time held the number five slot among the Top 100 Public Intellectuals. One dear lady commented afterward, "I had no idea there were so many atheists in Raleigh." Indeed.

For Hitchens, religion is the worst hoax ever perpetrated upon mankind. His case is "that religion's foundational books are transparent

---

[1]An earlier version of this preface appeared as "Atheism on the Rise?" in the *Biblical Recorder* 173, no. 14 (2007): 3.

fables, and that it is a man-made imposition, and that it has been an enemy of science and inquiry, and that it has subsisted largely on lies and fears, and been the accomplice of ignorance and guilt as well as of slavery, genocide, racism, and tyranny."[2] Hitchens charges religion with being "violent, irrational, intolerant, allied to racism and tribalism and bigotry, invested in ignorance and hostile to free inquiry, contemptuous of women and coercive toward children," and on top of it all, religion wishes "the destruction of the world."[3] He unapologetically decries Mother Teresa as a hypocrite, the Dalai Lama as deluded, Martin Luther King Jr. as a pretender, and Jesus as more or less immoral.

What unnerves me more than his shots at this or that saint is the fact that the stereotypes Hitchens presents of Christianity seem to resonate with people's experiences of Christianity. For too many people, Christianity comes off as this absurd idea that God killed his Son to pay for some violation against God's honor perpetrated by humans who were, for the most part, unaware of their trespasses. God demands that we accept this blood-letting as the only true path to eternal happiness. If we are sufficiently remorseful for our own unworthiness and confess, with ample groveling, our gratitude for God killing his Son, then we will be rewarded with eternal glory and power. If we decline the offer, we will be made to suffer the cruelest torture forever in the afterlife. Hitchens's portrayal is an exaggerated stereotype to be sure, but one that resonates with the real experience of many individuals.

It became clear from my exchange with Hitchens, and the countless comments, phone calls and emails I received afterward, that this book needed to be written. Not because the faith needs to be defended against the atheists, but because Christianity is at a crossroads—perhaps a crisis. The CUNY Graduate Center conducted a survey of American religious identity in 1990 and 2001, in which they randomly surveyed over 50,000 homes and found that, whereas in 1990, 90 percent of those surveyed identified themselves as religious, the number dropped to 81 percent in 2001.[4] More telling than a survey of attitudes is a sur-

---

[2]Christopher Hitchens, *God Is Not Great* (New York: Twelve, 2007), p. 229.
[3]Ibid., p. 56.
[4]For the full report, see "American Religious Identity Survey," The Graduate Center of the City

vey of pocketbooks. In a study published in 2008, Christian Smith, Michael Emerson and Patricia Snell demonstrate that fewer American Christians are donating generously to religious causes.[5] For various reasons, people are just not as motivated to give as once they were. Statistics and surveys alone do not suffice to make a case, but they are indicators. There seems to be for many people a general dissatisfaction with traditional church structures and habits. The appearance of the emerging church movement, the Ekklesia Project, Renovaré, the liturgical movement and alternative denominational arrangements especially among evangelicals testifies in part to this dissatisfaction. Tony Jones, one of the key spokespersons of the Emergent movement, bluntly states, "In the twenty-first century, it's not God who's dead. It's the church. Or at least conventional forms of church."[6]

Christianity must find new ways to articulate the faith of old—not only for the sake of the future, but for the sake of the church now. What the Christian community needs more than anything is a constructive creativity springing forth from the wealth of our long and distinguished tradition and from a genuine encounter with the living God of Jesus Christ. The Christian faith knows no children or grandchildren; belief can be instilled but it cannot be inherited. Each new generation must decide for the faith on its own. Each generation of Christians is potentially the last generation and so every generation is responsible for proclaiming the gospel to the next.

One thing needs to be made clear. The challenge before us is not one of making our religion relevant or "useful" to society. There are some among us who desperately want our presence to be seen as indispens-

---

University of New York <www.gc.cuny.edu/faculty/research_briefs/aris/key_findings.htm> (accessed October 7, 2008). Baylor University conducted a much smaller but perhaps more in-depth survey on this issue in 2005. Their results were perhaps a bit more positive. They found that 82 percent of their nearly two thousand respondents identified themselves as Christian, 70 percent pray regularly and nearly half attend church regularly. The full report can be found at "American Piety in the 21st Century," Baylor University <www.isreligion.org/research/surveys ofreligion/surveysofreligion.pdf> (accessed October 7, 2008).
[5]Christian Smith, Michael Emerson and Patricia Snell, *Passing the Plate: Why American Christians Don't Give Away More Money* (New York: Oxford University Press, 2008).
[6]Tony Jones, *The New Christians: Dispatches from the Emergent Frontier* (San Francisco: Jossey-Bass, 2008), p. 4.

able to civilization and valuable for the common good.[7] Too often it is thought that the best way to answer an atheist like Hitchens is to show him all the good religion can do, show him how relevant it is, show him how useful it can be. But in so doing, we forget the point of the gospel. The gospel is not meant to be useful to the world, but to save the world from all its uses and misuses. Christians have been given the ministry of reconciliation, not respectability. St. Paul said that this gospel stuff was going to look foolish and weak. The best thing Christians can do in the face of atheists is to *act like Christians*; the best thing the church can do in a world gone cold is to *act like the church*. But don't be fooled, it's is not as easy as it sounds.

This book presents the foolishness of the gospel as something to be taken seriously. It is an exercise in Christian thinking meant for flesh and blood—for mirror-fogging Christians. My prayer throughout this book is that our "conversation be always full of grace, seasoned with salt, so that you may know how to answer everyone" (Col 4:6).

I will not claim original ownership of any of the ideas here; they are the product of long conversations with friends and mentors, both living and laid low. Jesus said, "He who speaks on his own authority seeks his own glory" (Jn 7:18 RSV; see also Jn 12:49). I have certainly not spoken on my own authority; I am able to say what I say because of those who have gone before me. To them I owe a debt of gratitude. In particular, I want to thank the following people who helped guide and edit this work: my dad, Timothy Alexander, John Alford, Elizabeth Austin, Nathaniel Blake, Catherine Campbell, David Carter, Rodney Clapp, Steve Harmon, Barry Harvey, Jason Horrell, Glenn Jonas, Cameron Jorgenson, Christopher Kah, Kathy Lopez, Cody McCain, Ruth Quakenbush, Amanda Rodriguez, Daniel West, Brandon White, my colleagues in the NABPR-at-Large group and at Campbell University, my wife, Charissa, and my daughter, Cassidy. Finally, I want to thank Gary Deddo and the InterVarsity Press team. I am grateful that they believed in me and this work and have labored so that it might see the light of day.

---

[7]For example, see Stephen Prothero, *Religious Literacy: What Every American Needs to Know—And Doesn't* (New York: HarperCollins, 2007).

1

TO WHAT SHALL I
COMPARE IT?

The world is full of Christian truths run wild.

G. K. CHESTERTON

STARTING WITH JESUS

IN THE SYNOPTIC GOSPELS, when Jesus talks about what is nearest and dearest to him, he invariably talks about the kingdom of God. Surely the kingdom of God (or alternatively, "kingdom of heaven") is one of the central refrains of the Gospels. Jesus mentions it over one hundred times. All four Gospel writers record Jesus talking about it. Jesus sends his disciples out "to preach the kingdom of God" (Lk 9:2). In the first chapter of Acts we find the Lord, even after the resurrection, lingering forty days with his disciples in order to speak "about the kingdom of God" (Acts 1:3). And yet, as indisputably important as this theme is to Jesus' ministry and message, its meaning is not at all obvious, neither to the casual reader nor to the well-trained exegete.[1] As surprising as it sounds, Jesus never tells his followers point-blank: this is what the kingdom of God is and this is what it should do.

Instead, Jesus regularly asks, "What is the kingdom of God like?

---

[1] Joseph Fitzmyer, *Luke (I-IX)*, Anchor Bible Commentary, vol. 28 (New York: Doubleday, 1981), pp. 153-57.

What shall I compare it to?" (Lk 13:18). He does not respond by un-
curling an array of neat propositions defining and delimiting the kingdom. Rather he answers by way of "parables" (*parabolē*, in Greek).[2] "It
is like a mustard seed, which a man took and planted in his garden" and
"It is like yeast that a woman took and mixed into a large amount of
flour until it worked all through the dough" (Lk 13:19, 21). Elsewhere
he compares the kingdom of heaven to a treasure hidden in a field, a
merchant in search of fine pearls, a net thrown into the sea (Mt
13:44-50). But what do these comparisons *mean*? How do they help us
understand the kingdom of God?

One way to explain the figurative looseness of Jesus' statements is to
say that it reveals a lack of clarity on Jesus' part. Perhaps Jesus was uncertain about what he intended to say. Perhaps he had not thought it
through completely. Or, perhaps he simply lacked the capability to express his meaning in precise language. Could it be the case that Jesus
did not have enough words in his satchel to say what he really meant?
Did he fall back on parables and comparisons because he lacked the
means to articulate himself clearly?

I find these suggestions unacceptable. Jesus steps through the
pages of the Gospel as someone with a rock-solid grasp of his own
identity and mission. By the reactions of the crowds and the attrac-
tion of the disciples to his message, it is evident that his message *was*
clear and he *did* know how to communicate it with stark simplicity in
word and deed. I would contend that Jesus did not "fall back" on
analogies and parables. Like Horton the Elephant, Jesus meant what
he said and said what he meant. What he meant to say he said by way
of the parables, that is, little stories and comparisons. Both Matthew
and Mark confirm that Jesus "never" taught without using parables
(Mt 13:34; Mk 4:34).

Even so, not everyone "got" what Jesus was up to, including his own
disciples. At one point one of them scratched his sun-burnt head and
asked, "Why do you speak to the people in parables?" Good question.

---

[2]The Gospel word *parabolē* is best translated "parable," although it can also be rendered "similitude," "comparison" or even "proverb," drawing on its Hebrew predecessor *māšāl*: "maxim,"
"proverb," "obscure prophecy," "parable," "allegory" or "taunt." Fitzmyer, *Luke (I-IX)*, p. 600.

Jesus replied firmly and without equivocation,

> The reason I speak to them in parables is that "seeing they do not per-ceive, and hearing they do not listen, nor do they understand." With them indeed is fulfilled the prophecy of Isaiah that says: "You will in-deed listen, but never understand, you will indeed look, but never per-ceive." (Mt 13:10, 13-14 NRSV)

Odd way to answer a simple question. Does Jesus *want* to bam-boozle and frustrate his hearers? That hardly seems productive. But if we read further, we find that the rabbi from Galilee distinguishes be-tween having eyes to see and seeing, having ears to hear and listening, having a brain and understanding. "He who has ears, let him hear" (Mt 13:43). The things of God are not to be polished into tiny, shiny doodads that dazzle the eyes; they are not to be turned into pink feath-ers that tickle the ears. Rather they are meant for formation, for trans-formation, for the invigoration of new life. The kingdom of God is not a location on a map; it is not a set of facts that pop up on Wikipedia. "The kingdom of God does not come with your careful observation, nor will people say, 'Here it is,' or 'There it is,' because the kingdom of God is within you" (Lk 17:20-21). Other translations say the kingdom of God is "among you" (NRSV) or "in your midst" (TNIV, NASB) or "here with you" (CEV).[3]

The late nineteenth century author of *War and Peace*, Leo Tolstoy, wrote a provocative political treatise advocating nonviolent resistance against the atrocities of the oppressive Russian regime titled *"The King-dom of God Is Within You": Christianity Not as a Mystic Religion but as a New Theory of Life*.[4] Even his title offers an important insight about the meaning of the verse in question: to deny that the kingdom of God is a *thing* that can be observed is not necessarily to reduce it to a mystic re-ligion, inconsequential for life on the ground. Rather, saying the king-dom of God is among you, in you and around you is a way of saying that it reorients you from the inside out. It is a new theory of life. The king-

---

[3]Like the NIV, the KJV, NKJV and ASV say "within you."

[4]Leo Tolstoy, *"The Kingdom of God Is Within You": Christianity Not as a Mystic Religion but as a New Theory of Life* (Rockville, Md.: Wildside Press, 2007).

dom of heaven is not something we observe from a distance, but something that upends us, impinges upon our allegiances, files new citizenship papers on us. It is not a question of eyes and ears, but of seeing and hearing.

Jesus' parabolic presentation of the kingdom of God highlights something important about the nature of the Christian faith in general: it cannot be *quantified*, only *qualified*. It is not a quantity of information, nor is it a particular type of experience. Anyone can learn trivial facts about a religion; anyone can claim experience with God, or the archangel Michael, or Moroni, or Mother Nature, or whatever. The Christian faith requires a *qualitative* discernment of information and experience. First John warns us not to believe every spirit or experience, but to "test the spirits to see whether they are from God" (1 Jn 4:1). This qualitative testing is wisdom. St. Augustine (354–430), who departed as a young man from the provincial North African town of Thagaste to become one of the most influential theologians of all time, concurs. Awareness "of things divine is properly called wisdom, and of things human is properly given the name knowledge."[5]

What we seek here is wisdom *of* the faith, not simply knowledge *about* the faith. Knowledge about the faith is external, empirical and impersonal; it can be typed up in bullet points and published on the Web for anyone to read. Wisdom of the faith is internal, transformative and communal; it is not open to just any inquiring mind—it must be experienced by the open heart so that "the Spirit himself testifies with our spirit" (Rom 8:16).

I do not wish to diminish the importance of knowledge *about* religions and practices and beliefs. There is a place and a time for acquiring information, history and statistics. Statements about religions must be supported by facts, and a firm grasp of the facts is indispensable to wisdom and understanding. Misunderstandings usually occur when there is a misrepresentation of the facts or an ignorance of the facts. Nevertheless, information about a religion, a system of belief or a worldview can only get one so far. *How do we talk about the faith we live?*

---

[5]Augustine *The Trinity* 14.1, trans. Edmund Hill (Brooklyn, N.Y.: New City Press, 1991), p. 371.

How do we talk about the internal, transformative and communal elements of its wisdom? How is the mystery of the faith communicated?

WHAT CHRISTIANITY IS LIKE

At a critical moment in the 1999 movie *The Matrix*, Laurence Fishburne's character, Morpheus, leans forward in his leather chair and asks a wide-eyed Keanu Reeves if he wants to know what the Matrix is. Neo, Reeves's character, nods his head yes, to which Morpheus responds cryptically, "Unfortunately, no one can be told what the Matrix is. You have to see it for yourself." The same could be said of the Christian faith: you have to see it for yourself.[6] No one can be told *what* Christianity is, at least not fully and completely. I will nonetheless make an attempt in this book to sketch things out. My intention is not to tell what Christianity is, but to show *what it is like*. By way of his parables, Jesus taught his disciples how to compare the kingdom of heaven with the things of this world. In my own limited way, I want to follow this example and show what the Christian faith is like through comparisons with the things of this world. By considering the things most familiar to us, we will hopefully catch a glimpse of the things of God.

Intellectual modesty is not the only reason for choosing this course of action. Making concrete and earthy comparisons, rather than pontificating abstractly and eruditely about what the Christian religion must essentially be, brings us nearer to the heart of mystery and the joy of faith. The now-retired Cambridge theologian Nicholas Lash, comments:

> The language that we use, the terminology that we employ, does not become less anthropomorphic, less sprung from earthly soil, by becoming more abstract, rarefied, or technical. If anything, something more like the opposite is the case: the entire Bible bears witness to the fact

---

[6]Ludwig Wittgenstein (*Philosophical Investigations*, 3rd ed., trans. G. E. M. Anscombe [New York: Macmillan, 1958], p. 61) might add that the moment of "seeing it" *is* the moment of understanding, the attainment of wisdom:

> Try not to think of understanding as a "mental process" at all.—For *that* is the expression which confuses you. But ask yourself: in what sort of case, in what kind of circumstances, do we say, "Now I know how to go on," when, that is, the formula *has* occurred to me?—
> In the sense in which there are processes (including mental processes) which are characteristic of understanding, understanding is not a mental process.

that the imagery of the poet and the storyteller is better fitted than the abstractions of the philosopher to express the relations that obtain between the Holy One and the creation which He convenes and calls into His presence.[7]

As Lash observes, it is not necessarily an improvement to leave behind earth-born language for more spiritual and philosophical words. St. Paul says, "unless you speak intelligible words with your tongue, how will anyone know what you are saying? You will just be speaking into the air" (1 Cor 14:9).

Too often we find ourselves speaking into the air. This is a perennial problem. Christians have always struggled to put into intelligible words what Christ and their faith in Christ means. Christians have never had at their disposal "heavenly words" or magic wands or saintly supercomputers that might explain everything at a single stroke. We have had to bend and stretch and sometimes break human words. It is rightly said that

> the prophets uttered the Word; Jesus incarnated it. Still, God did not provide them with any heavenly language, syntax, or grammar; to express themselves they had to strain their ingenuity to twist borrowed words and phrases. Thus, as soon as it appeared in Palestine, the theology of biblical revelation was as halting as Jacob after his struggle with the angel. It suffered from a disproportion between what it was supposed to announce on behalf of God and the means at its disposal for saying something to men.[8]

The disproportion is great indeed. Undoubtedly there will be much straining of ingenuity and borrowing of words and phrases in this book. And, at certain points, every comparison and example presented in this book will break down. No analogy is perfect. The fear of the Lord is the beginning of wisdom and the fear of overreaching ourselves is the beginning of theology. And so, we will tread lightly and with humility—exploring but not overstepping, boldly attending the banquet but not devouring everything on the table, engineering analogies but not

---

[7]Nicholas Lash, *Holiness, Speech, and Silence* (Burlington, Vt.: Ashgate, 2004), p. 15.
[8]Gabriel Widmer, quoted in Henri de Lubac, *The Christian Faith* (San Francisco: Ignatius Press, 1986), p. 267.

forgetting that they are just that, analogies.⁹ This word of caution being spoken, I want to borrow from four different fields in an attempt to present four different analogies in this remix of theology.

First, I want to argue that Christianity is like a *story*—with scenery, characters and plots—that reaches its climax in the person of Jesus the Christ, the main character who ties the plot together and gives it meaning.

Second, Christianity is like a *language*, with all the features and peculiarities thereof. We articulate the faith best when we learn the correct vocabulary and grammar to carry out the conversation.

Third, Christianity is like a *game*, with rules, players, goals and equipment for play. Each of these elements carries with it its own implications for the practice of the Christian faith.

Fourth, Christianity is like a *culture*, in that it presents a distinct way of living, working, playing, worshiping, marrying and caring for the dead. Like a culture it is community based, and, also like a culture, it is learned through the long process of cultivation.

These four analogies are rich in theological discoveries and parabolic insights. When nurtured, they will yield a bright harvest. And yet, already we must pause to address three important concerns.

1. Why these four comparisons and not more? Or less? Or different

---

⁹Throughout this book, I use *analogy, likeness, resemblance* and *comparison* interchangeably; at the same time, I avoid *metaphor* and *symbol*. Although all these terms may sound synonymous, they are not. There are important differences. The comparisons in this book between games, languages, stories and cultures are not necessarily Christian *metaphors* (or at least that is not how I am employing them) and certainly not Christian *symbols*. Analogies make surface-level comparisons between two things and can help us draw out the inner structure and order of the things being compared. Metaphors, signs and symbols arise from the inner structures themselves and are intrinsic to the order of things. So, for instance, the cross, communion and baptism are not analogies, but symbols. The meaning of the cross is embedded in the symbol itself, and so is irreplaceable. The cross not only identifies and represents the Christian message; it is identified *with* the Christian message. In her classic study, Janet Martin Soskice goes to great lengths to distinguish between analogies, similes, metaphors, symbols and other tropes. Janet Martin Soskice, *Metaphor and Religious Language* (New York: Clarendon, 1985, 2002), pp. 54-66. Also see Colin Gunton, *The Actuality of the Atonement* (New York: T & T Clark, 1988, 2008); C. M. Turbayne, *The Myth of Metaphor* 2nd ed. (Columbia: University of South Carolina Press, 1970); Robert Masson, "The Force of Analogy," *Anglican Theological Review* 87, no. 3 (2005): 471-86; Robert Sokolowski, *The God of Faith and Reason: Foundation of Christian Theology* (Notre Dame, Ind.: University of Notre Dame Press, 1982); Carl Vaught, *Metaphor, Analogy, and the Place of Places: Where Religion and Philosophy Meet* (Waco, Tex.: Baylor University Press, 2004).

ones altogether? To some readers, these four lenses for looking at the Christian faith may appear arbitrary or obscure. Hopefully the rationale for these four comparisons will become evident in the discussion of each. I do not deny that other comparisons could and perhaps should be made. Christianity is also a family, a nation, a university, an art, a banquet, a wedding party, a marriage, a concert, a journey, an orchard, a birth, an adoption, an errand and on and on.

But wait. "And on and on"? An immediate concern should be raised about "and on and on." The phrase seems to suggest there is no end or limit to the analogies that could be proposed. Would just any comparison work? Is Christianity anything someone wants to make it? No, certainly not. But the Spirit of Christ is forever teaching us "new tongues," calling us to new fields of harvest, and making us new men and women. Therefore, our ways of understanding and communicating the faith will be forever growing, changing and adjusting. Even so, there is an all-important criterion for these enterprises: namely Jesus Christ himself, Lord of heaven and earth, light of the world, supreme judge, head of the body of Christ, firstborn of the dead, pioneer and perfecter of our faith, the way, the truth and the life. With the ancient Byzantine hymn *Monogenēs*, we cry out,

> Only-begotten Son and Word of God, who being immortal yet didst deign for our salvation to be incarnate of the holy Mother of God and Ever-Virgin Mary, and without change didst become man and wast crucified, Christ our God, and by death didst overcome death, being One of the Holy Trinity and glorified together with the Father and the Holy Spirit: *Save us.*[10]

All our analogies and ways fall under the shadow of the cross. *Save us.* All things must be subjugated to the Son of God crucified for the sins of the world. *Save us.* To the questions—Could there be more analogies? Should there be less?—the answer is both: living faith will always blossom new understandings and insights, and so there will always be more images, comparisons and analogies. But at the same time,

---

[10]Emphasis mine. Quoted from Geoffrey Wainwright, *Doxology: The Praise of God in Worship, Doctrine, and Life* (New York: Oxford University Press, 1980), p. 53.

every analogy must come back to the one and only point of comparison, the revelation of God in Christ.[11]

2. A second important question is: What does it mean to say Christianity is "like" a narrative, a language, a game and a culture? Exactly *what kind* of comparison is being drawn between the faith and these other spheres of life? The extent of the comparisons will differ from analogy to analogy. However, I do think that Christianity does compare naturally to these four. To adopt an insight from the Austrian-born philosopher of logic and language, Ludwig Wittgenstein (1889–1951), we might say that the relationship between the different analogies presented here is one of "family resemblances." Just as "the various resemblances between members of a family: build, features, colour of eyes, gait, temperament, etc. etc. overlap and criss-cross," so also Christianity bears a likeness to storylines, languages, games and cultures.[12] There is a family resemblance. An individual is a combination of both parents, so that she looks and acts to a greater or lesser degree like mom and dad, but the child is not an identical copy of either parent. Family resemblance can be observed and described, but it cannot be pinpointed and defined with finality.[13] In the same way, Christianity tells the grand *story* of salvation, but it also enacts that story and puts it into practice. Christianity can be learned and spoken like a *language*, but it is more than linguistics. Christianity resembles the rules and logic of a *game*, but that does not make it identical to a game. Christianity lives like a *society*, but it also transcends the bounds of every human society.

Put differently, I hope to show that these four analogies are "fitting" of the Christian faith. There is a natural fit here. Something that is "fitting" not only functions properly but is also aesthetically pleasing and appropriate. Anselm (c. 1033–1109), the one-time bishop of Canterbury, opens his masterful *Cur Deus Homo* by observing "how fitting it is that the restoration of mankind has been brought about" by the

---

[11]See Thaleia's discourse in Methodius's *Banquet of the Ten Virgins*, in The Ante-Nicene Fathers (hereafter ANF), ed. Alexander Roberts and James Donaldson (Peabody, Mass.: Hendrickson, 1885, 2004), vol. 6, especially pp. 316-19.

[12]Wittgenstein, *Philosophical Investigations*, p. 32.

[13]Ibid.

incarnation, death and resurrection of Christ.[14] We can go back further in the record to find Athanasius (298–373), another soul like Anslem destined for great things (as a boy on the sandy shore of Alexandria he played the role of bishop over his more or less acquiescent playmates), extolling the work of God in the incarnation of the Word in Christ as "fit" and "fitting," "right and natural."[15] There is a longstanding theological tradition of highlighting the natural, aesthetic and pleasing nature of God's activity. Like a shirt that hangs just right on the shoulders and through the chest and arms, so these four analogies fit Christian belief and action. Are there other analogies that also fit? Of course. But for the present we will occupy ourselves with these four.

3. Shouldn't we acknowledge that Christianity is in many ways *not* like a story, a language, a game or a culture? Shouldn't we be careful and conscientious to acknowledge the limits of our comparisons? Yes and amen! Christianity *is* like a story, a language, a game and a culture, but it is also *unlike* those things. Not a single one of these comparisons says it all. Anselm, whom we have already introduced, was fond of relating God's work in creation to the careful craftsman's work in producing a piece of furniture. Creation shows signs of planning, ordering, shaping and arranging, just like a fine piece of furniture. It is the work of a divine Craftsman. Here is where things get strange. As soon as Anselm's analogy between the Creator and the craftsman gets off the ground, he stops, rethinks and changes directions: "I spy, however, a lot of unlikeness in this likeness."[16] Immediately Anselm begins to deconstruct his analogy, showing the ways in which God's labor is *unlike* that of a craftsman. "A craftsman can only imagine bodily things on the basis of things he has already come across. . . . But what did [God] draw upon?"[17] The comparison ends before it has a chance to flourish. Surprisingly, however, this does not defuse and defeat Anselm's point, but instead invigorates it. By highlighting the *unlikeness*, he presents all the

[14]Anselm of Canterbury, "Why God Became Man," *The Major Works* (New York: Oxford University Press, 1998), p. 268.
[15]Athanasius *On the Incarnation* sect. 1, 26, 44 (Crestwood, N.Y.: St. Vladimir's Seminary Press, 2000), pp. 25, 56, 80.
[16]Anselm, *Major Works*, pp. 24-25.
[17]Anselm *Monologion* sect. 11.

more clearly what kind of Creator we are dealing with, and how God's creation is radically different from any human creation.

Anselm's example teaches us that we need not shy away from the limitations of our comparisons; we need not try to force every comparison to fit perfectly nor do we need to hide the parts that do not fit. Instead, we need to be aware that the best lessons might be found as much in the mismatch as in the match.

The contention of this book is simple: the best way to understand what Christianity *is* is to find out what it is *like*, to compare it to things with which we are familiar. To the question, What is Christianity? this book responds: the question needs to be answered by means of images, similes, comparisons and analogies.[18] To that end, let us put on our ears for hearing and our eyes for seeing and find out what awaits us.

---

[18]"The question you ask needs to be answered by means of an image or simile." Plato *Republic* 488a, trans. G. M. A. Grube (Indianapolis: Hackett, 1992), p. 161.

CHRISTIANITY

AS STORY

2

CHRISTIANITY AS STORY

Come then, clear thyself of all the prepossessions which occupy thy mind,

and throw off the habit which leadeth thee astray, and become a new man,

as it were, from the beginning, as one who would listen to a new story.

EPISTLE TO DIOGNETUS

LET US BEGIN WITH STORIES. Christianity bears a strong "family resemblance," as Wittgenstein would say, to a story. That almost goes without saying. In the beginning, God created the world. Because of sin and for the sake of salvation, God sent his Son into the world to rescue the world he had created. In the end, God will resurrect, redeem and recreate that world. In that quick snapshot, we have presented the drama of Christianity, complete with characters, setting and conflict as well as a beginning, middle and end. Let us identify some of the points of comparison between stories and the Christian faith.

✛ Comparing Christianity to a story is rewarding because when we think about Christianity as a story, we naturally begin to identify *main* characters and *main* events, and we see how those characters and events fit together. The Bible is full of names and events. Readers need ways of mentally organizing and ordering those names and events. Reading the Bible as a holistic story can help them in that task.

✚ Thinking about Christianity as a story helps believers connect the biblical witness with the historic development of the church and with the life of the church today. When we understand Christianity as one big story, we do not divide the Bible from church history, and both of those from the practice of Christianity today. Rather, we understand that it is all one grand narrative of God's love and provision and calling. We understand that all of history, including the Bible, and including the church today, are part of the story.

✚ Not only do we identify *main* characters and events in the Bible and in church history, we begin to identify *our* role as characters in God's story. Sometimes we struggle to see where our individual lives fit into God's greater plan. But when we consider our lives as part of God's story, then we see that we all have a role to play in it.

✚ If Christianity is a story, then it has a beginning, a middle and an end. Becoming aware of this truth can give us hope, especially when the woes of the world drag us down. Christianity is not stagnant, it is not stationary, nothing ever remains the same; *the story directs our attention to the future.* Christianity has a *telos*, that is, an end, a goal, a consummation and fulfillment. *Resurrection, judgment, new creation, heaven, kingdom of God*—these are all biblical words that remind us of this fact. Christianity is like a story in the sense that its plot is driving towards a resolution, or, to use the language of the theologians, Christianity is eschatological in nature. The story has an Author with a master plan.

The makeup of a story offers a fruitful and natural comparison with the makeup of the Christian faith. We have briefly highlighted four points of likeness (and we admit that each of these points could be filled out in detail and others added). However, Christianity is also *unlike* a story in some equally important ways. As Anselm would say, I spy a lot of unlikeness in this likeness. It is proper that we also make note of the points of disparity.

▬ If we are not careful, the analogy of story can make us theologically naive and spiritually insensitive. If we treat the analogy in an overly simplistic way, we can trap ourselves in an unholy determinism. If history is one big story that God has written from eternity, then whatever happens *must* be right. It's all part of the story—the good, the bad and the ugly. There is no reason to object to anything that happens—cancer, car wrecks, fires, wars. There is no reason to pray for anything different. God has already written the story of what must happen. Either I am one of the elect or damned, and there is nothing I can do to change my fate in the drama.

■ On a similar note, how can I help but see myself as a minor character in this story? If we push the comparison between Christianity and story too far, we might find it hard to see how we are involved in or responsible for this story. If the body of Christ on earth, which encompasses some two billion people today, is a grand narrative of God's work, does anything I do or say matter? Here, at the point of personal involvement, we see a potential weakness of the story analogy.

■ When we relate Christianity to storytelling, we must avoid giving the impression that it is "just" a story. The gospel is not "just" a good or cute or interesting story. It is not just a true story, in point of fact. Christianity claims not just to tell a story, but to change lives. By no means do we want to deflate the power of the gospel by reducing it to the level of "just" a story.

■ This third point leads to a final question: What *kind* of story is Christianity? Christianity can be modeled or described in story terms, but when we try to name or classify it *as a story*, we see the analogy begin to break down. For instance, is the Christian story a legend or a fairytale? Obviously not. It is not a work of fiction but fact. However, even the word "fact" is not quite sufficient to explain what kind of truth the gospel presents. Christianity claims to be more than a reporting of historical facts; it claims to be the way to relationship with the divine Creator of the universe. Modern theologians have struggled mightily with the dilemma: What kind of story is it? Karl Barth suggested that since Christian gospel offers much more than history, perhaps it could be described as a "non-historical history." Hardly an improvement. He later proposed to call it a "saga."[1] C. S. Lewis put forward the label "myth," with the added bonus that Christianity is a *real* myth, or a myth that actually happened.[2] Again, hardly an improvement. The fact that "myth" needs to be immediately qualified as *true* and *real* should indicate a problem with the word from the beginning.

The trouble with "saga" and "myth" is that even when they are qualified and clarified by the great minds of Barth and Lewis, they are still freighted with more baggage than they are worth. They still imply, whether they want to or not, that the tale is fabricated, not to be trusted—it is a myth, a saga. I would suggest that the problem is not one of word choice, but of analogy. Christianity can be *described* in terms of a story, but it cannot be *categorized* as one. It does not fit into a subset or class of stories; it cannot be placed into the genre of myth, saga, history, non-historical history, meta-narrative, fable, or theatrical drama. To the question, What kind of story is Christianity?, the best answer is, None. It is not a *type* of story, it is *like* a story. Here is where the resemblance ends.

---

[1]Karl Barth, *Church Dogmatics* 3.1, trans. J. W. Edwards et al. (Edinburgh: T & T Clark, 1958), pp. 80-87.
[2]C. S. Lewis, *God in the Dock*, ed. Walter Hooper (Grand Rapids: Eerdmans, 1970), pp. 63-67.

3

CHRISTIANITY AS STORY

CREATIONS AND CATASTROPHES

THE LITERARY GIANT ERNEST HEMINGWAY was once challenged to write a story using only six words. He responded with this, "For sale: baby shoes, never used." Other famous authors have been asked to do the same. John Updike wrote, "'Forgive me!' 'What for?' 'Never mind.'" A six word account of Christianity might be: Creation, Catastrophe, Covenant, Christ, Church, Consummation.[1] This basic plotline unfolds in Scripture like a six-act drama.

Act one opens with the setting and the main characters of the drama. The setting is earth, the main characters are God and humanity, the story is their relationship. Act two introduces the conflict and the crisis that propels the action forward. A rift opens up between God and humanity—a "great divorce" that shatters the relationship. Act three shows the first attempt at resolving the conflict, God's covenant with the Hebrew people. The action comes to a head in Act four, the climax of the story. God and humanity are brought together and united in one person, Jesus the Christ, the Son of Man who is also the Son of God. A new relationship and a new covenant are forged. Act five tells how that new relationship is lived out by the new people of God, the church. Act six is not so much the *end* of the story, but where the telling of the story ends. All things are consummated and made as they were in-

---

[1]This six-part drama has been identified by numerous theologians, including Stanley Hauerwas, N. T. Wright, Barry Harvey, Rodney Clapp, Craig Bartholomew and Michael Goheen.

tended to be, including the relationship of God to humanity and humanity to God. This final act is already in production and waiting to be performed.

ACT 1: CREATION

The first act of the drama is creation. What was God doing before creation? The well-worn joke is, "Preparing a place in hell for people who ask that question!" Augustine cites this wry retort in his own treatment of the issue—only to reprimand anyone who would dare to use it. He instead recommends that we answer with candidness: "I would rather have answered, 'What I do not know, I do not know,' than have cracked a joke that exposed a serious questioner to ridicule and won applause for giving an untrue answer."[2] What God was working on before creation is something about which no one can possibly know, so we should simply admit our ignorance and move on. Creation is where the narration begins. What happened before that is not pertinent to the story. Creation gives us the setting (the universe, earth) and the main characters (God and humanity). *Who is this God and who are these humans?* These are the questions the first chapters of Genesis are answering.

In the opening chapters of Genesis we find ourselves in a primordial past, in a faraway place—Eden. There we encounter Adam and Eve and Cain and Abel, whom we recognize from brightly colored Renaissance frescoes. Their two dimensional bodies and expressionless faces peer down on us from curved cathedral ceilings, whispering of things known when the earth was young. These chapters can be hard for modern readers to hear and reconcile. It is important, as a way of catching hold of its message, to look not only at Genesis, nor only at Genesis in comparison with modern science, but at Genesis in comparison with other ancient creation accounts from the Fertile Crescent—the region spanning from Egypt, through Canaan and Syria, to Mesopotamia and Babylon (modern day Iraq and Iran).

A number of competing accounts of origins in circulation during the

---

[2]Augustine *Confessions* 11.14, trans. Maria Boulding (Hyde Park, N.Y.: New City Press, 1997), p. 294.

time when the Genesis account was being transmitted orally and in writing. One such story from the civilizations of the Fertile Crescent is the *Enuma Elish*, not discovered until the late 1800s even though it dates back thousands of years.[3] It was known and recited in places like Ur of the Chaldeans, where Abraham, Lot and Sarah grew up.

The account begins with Apsu, the freshwater god, and Tiamat, the saltwater goddess, "mixing their waters" to procreate. Their divine offspring turn out to be, like most children, loud and obnoxious. Father Apsu plans to rid himself of them, but the younger gods get wind of the plan and kill him first. They congratulate themselves for their cunning. However, their pre-emptive strike overlooked something—Tiamat, Apsu's beloved. Mother Tiamat's rage swells against her children and she bends her will to their destruction. Everyone scatters at the sight of Tiamat. What can be done to quell the pounding waves of Tiamat's fury? Finally Marduk, one of the children, agrees to stand up to her on the condition that if he is victorious he will be declared king. Marduk boldy ventures out to face Tiamat and the sea monsters she has created for battle. He casts a net over Tiamat and her army, but Tiamat opens her strong saltwater mouth and begins sucking Marduk into a watery death. The young warrior feels his feet slipping as he tries to resist her pull. At the last moment, when he can resist no more, Marduk pulls an arrow from his quiver and fires. The arrow pops the swollen Tiamat like a balloon. Marduk then proceeds to split her in half. From her corpse he fashions the world as we know it and from the blood and bone of Kingu, Tiamat's new mate who is also slain, he molds humans to be foot-servants of the gods.

The *Enuma Elish* is an amazing story, though obviously not a scientific account; it does not concern itself with modern scientific questions. So perhaps we should throw it out. If we discard it because it is obviously mythical, we miss the real significance of the story. Instead, if we can put aside our scientific, historical concerns for a moment and

[3]Philippe Talon, ed., *The Standard Babylonian Creation Myth: Enūma Eliš* (Helsinki: University of Helsinki Neo-Assyrian Text Corpus Project, 2005); W. G. Lambert, *Enūma Eliš* (Oxford: Clarendon Press, 1966); Alexander Heidel, *The Babylonian Genesis: The Story of the Creation* (Chicago: University of Chicago Press, 1951), p. 129. Heidel makes a fascinating comparison of the Genesis account and *Enuma Elish*.

allow this ancient story to speak on its own terms, we find that it answers two basic questions: Who are the gods? Who are the humans? These are the questions the Chaldeans and Babylonians were asking.

Who are the gods for these ancient people? Most obviously, we observe there is more than one. The gods are many in number, and they show themselves to be selfish. Apsu wants to kill his children because they irritate him; Marduk will only fight Tiamat on the condition that he be named king. In addition, the gods are prone to violence. They create the world out of death and humankind out of spilled blood. Who are the humans? They are slaves of the gods and subject to their disposal. This story also explains why humans tend toward violence and why they are aggressive, because they were made out of violence and death.

In Genesis the picture is strikingly different. Who is God? "In the beginning when God created the heavens and the earth . . ." (Gen 1:1). There is only one God instead of many. This God, by the way, does not represent any particular natural force like water or fire or air, but stands above and outside of natural forces. How does this God create? Not by fighting or forcing or having sex, but simply by speaking. "And God said, 'Let there be light'; and there was light" (Gen 1:3). His words alone bring order out of chaos and life out of nothing. Second Esdras, a late-first-century Jewish writing, restates this truth beautifully:

> O Lord, you spoke at the beginning of creation, and said on the first day, "Let heaven and earth be made," and your word accomplished the work. Then the spirit was blowing, and darkness and silence embraced everything; the sound of human voices was not yet there. Then you commanded a ray of light to be brought out from your store-chambers, so that your works could be seen. (2 Esd 6:38-40)

Let there be light so that the works of God can be seen. The God of Genesis speaks a word of goodness over his works: "God saw all that he had made, and it was very good" (Gen 1:31). The world is not made out of selfishness and violence, but out of goodness. It is good in itself.

Who are the humans? Here also we find contrast with the *Enuma Elish*. "Then God said, 'Let us make man in our image, in our likeness; and let them rule over the fish of the sea, and the birds of the air, over the livestock, over all the wild animals of the earth, and over all the creatures that move along the ground'" (Gen 1:26). Humans are formed not out of violence, but in God's very likeness; not to be the slaves of the gods, but to enjoy and rule over creation, like God himself.

To what can this *image of God* refer? When we look in the mirror, we see something of God. What in us reflects the Creator? Any number of answers could be given at this point. Some say the image of God refers to our sense of right and wrong. Humans have a sense of morality not shared with other animals. There is only one problem with this suggestion: were humans created originally with this sense of right and wrong? Let us remember, the tree of the knowledge of good and evil was the tree the humans were *not* supposed to taste; the responsibility of morality falls under the curse. Other theologians suggest instead that the image of God is found in human reason. Humans can think rationally in a way unlike other animals.

There are many potential answers to the riddle: what *is* the image of God? To what does it refer?[4] I argue that what we mirror about God is most probably linked to the purpose for which we were created. The Christian tradition affirms that humans were created for the purpose of relationship with God. The story of Christianity is one of God's relationship with humanity. As such, the image of God refers (at the very least) to a deep-felt desire arising from our very nature, from our inmost being, for relationship with our Creator.[5] We can only have true communication and genuine relationship with beings essentially like ourselves. Most dog owners would say they have a real relationship with their pet. But in truth, your relationship with your dog is rather one-directional. Your dog would just as soon sniff another dog as sit on your lap. You can have more of a relationship with a dog than with a pet rock, to be sure, but a truly intimate relationship can only be had with another human being, another creature like yourself. Likewise, God could not have authentic relationships with us if we were no more than

---

[4]A recently republished classic survey of this topic is Jürgen Moltmann, *On Human Being: Christian Anthropology in Conflicts of the Present* (Minneapolis: Fortress, 2009).

[5]There is a long and complicated history connected with the issue of "natural desire" for God. For the best and most rewarding treatment, see Henri de Lubac, *The Mystery of the Supernatural*, trans. Rosemary Sheed (New York: Crossroad, 1998).

dogs or rocks to God. And this is the amazing thing: we are not God's pets or God's rocks or God's robots; we can experience real relationship with our maker.

To have relationship with God means, most basically, that in some essential way we must be enough *like* God to relate to and communicate *with* God. The eighth Psalm ponders this amazing truth:

> When I consider your heavens,
>   the work of your fingers,
>   the moon and the stars,
>   which you have set in place,
> what is man that you are mindful of him,
>   the son of man that you care for him?
> You made him a little lower than the heavenly beings
>   and crowned him with glory and honor. (Ps 8:3-5)

We were created for community, for fellowship with our Creator. Augustine is right when he observes that "to praise you is the desire of man, a little piece of your creation. You stir man to take pleasure in praising you, because you have made us for yourself."[6] Thomas Aquinas (1225–1274) adds that "all things stretch out to be assimilated by God."[7] All creation longs to return to its source, to know its maker. We are made with the capacity and the desire to know God.

David Bentley Hart, the sublimely erudite Eastern Orthodox theologian, notes that this proclivity toward relationship with the divine is not a defect of the creation, but the expression of creaturely freedom. "To be free is to be able to flourish as the kind of being one is, and so to attain the ontological good toward which one's nature is oriented."[8] We humans are freest when we are fulfilling our inmost desire, which means when we are in step with our Creator and when we are living up to the image in which we were made. Hart's Christian conception of

---

[6] Augustine *Confessions* 1.1, trans. Henry Chadwick (New York: Oxford University Press, 1991), p. 3.

[7] This is John Sullivan's translation of *Summa contra Gentiles* 3.19. John Sullivan, "Matter for Heaven: Blondel, Christ and Creation," *Ephremerides Theologicae Lovanienses* 64 (1988): 60-83. For an earlier use of this idea, see Gregory of Nyssa, "On the Soul and the Resurrection," Nicene and Post-Nicene Fathers (hereafter NPNF), 2nd series, vol. 5, p. 112.

[8] David B. Hart, *The Doors of the Sea* (Grand Rapids: Eerdmans, 2005), p. 71.

freedom rubs against our ordinary, modern definitions of freedom. Usually we tend to think of freedom as the ability to choose either this or that arbitrarily, the right to do or not do something independent of all constraints. In a Christian understanding freedom is not a neutral right. There is only one possible act of freedom: *choosing God*, which implies the choice for the image of God within us, the choice for our own human purpose and destiny.

Rejecting relationship with God is not an act of free will, but the destruction of freedom, the corruption of choice. "The will that chooses poorly . . . has not thereby become freer, but has further enslaved itself to those forces that prevent it from achieving its full expression."[9] When we choose against God, we forfeit our freedom. Paul is crystal clear on this point: we become "slaves to sin" and the result is death (Rom 6:16-23; Gal 3:22; 4:3). Athanasius of Alexandria (299–373) describes it as "throwing away [our] birthright."[10] Indeed, choosing against God is not an expression of "choice" but the chaining of choice, the forgoing of freedom, the injuring of self and the disruption of the created harmony.

ACT 2: CATASTROPHE

The second act introduces conflict, the dilemma that propels the action forward. In the second act, the relationship between Creator and creation fractures and fragments, not due to "irreconcilable differences" but to unfaithfulness on the part of the humans. Genesis 3 relates the dark story of original disobedience. The woman and her husband partake of fruit from a forbidden tree, which until this point had been dropping its produce, ripe with the knowledge of good and evil, onto the grassy floor beneath its branches, untouched. Not only do they disobey, they become aroused to an awareness of good and evil, desire and shame, honesty and deception. They realize they are naked and hide their bodies, they deny responsibility for what they have done and are banished from the garden.

---

[9]Hart, *Doors*, p. 71.
[10]Athanasius *On the Incarnation* 3 (Crestwood, N.Y.: St. Vladimir's Seminary Press, 2000), p. 29.

In this rich and complicated story of "the Fall," the man and the woman alienate themselves from their Creator, from one another, and from the land out of which they came. *Sin*, the word which Christians use for this alienation, is not just a mistake in calculation or an error in judgment, it is a willful breaking of trust. It is a rebellion. The catastrophe is that we refuse the Holy One's stunning offer of relationship. Not only that, sin means that we also refuse our own nature, purpose and destiny—the image in which we were fashioned. Athanasius, around the bright age of twenty or twenty-five, wrote these profound words about the effects of sin:

> But men, having turned from the contemplation of God to evil of their own devising, had come inevitably under the law of death. Instead of remaining in the state in which God had created them, they were in process of becoming corrupted entirely, and death had them completely under its dominion. For the transgression of the commandment was making them turn back again according to their nature; and as they had at the beginning come into being out of non-existence, so were they now on the way to returning, through corruption, to non-existence again. The presence and love of the Word had called them into being; inevitably, therefore when they lost the knowledge of God, they lost existence with it.[11]

Not only does the catastrophe cost us our knowledge of God, it costs us our very existence, purpose and calling. Sinning causes us to sink back towards nonexistence and death. "The soul who sins is the one who will die" (Ezek 18:20). "Then, after desire has conceived, it gives birth to sin; and sin, when it is full-grown, gives birth to death" (Jas 1:15).

Why did humanity disobey God's good command? Why do we sin? Any attempt to ferret out the motivation for sinning only leaves one perplexed. Sin is always unplanned, unbelievable, ineffectual and stupid. There is never a *good* reason to sin. The very idea of disobedience and sin is *absurd*. Sin does not make sense: it does not make sense to rebel against our maker and refuse to accept our own nature. First John says, "For

---

[11]Ibid., 4, pp. 29-30.

everything in the world—the cravings of sinful man, the lust of his eyes and the boasting of what he has and does—comes not from the Father but from the world" (1 Jn 2:16). Sin is not from the Father. "No one who lives in him keeps on sinning" (1 Jn 3:6). Sin is what went wrong; it goes *against* God's will, it is unnatural. Augustine says, "if sin is natural, there is no such thing as sin."[12] God does not make room for our rebellion, God does not bless sin as "okay"—God sends the Son to snatch us from the jaws of sin and death. God's creation is good and orderly and sin is the intentional shattering of that goodness, the inexplicable disordering of that order. Sin means shooting oneself in the foot; it is our own self-destruction. Sin is humanity's baffling refusal of good will. It cannot be explained, classified and filed away as if it were all part of the plan. Sin does not fit; it never merits a *good* reason; it is not an act of free will, but the refusal of freedom and of our very nature.

My wife and I were once part of a church that worked closely with inner-city kids. The church raised money to send a select number of them to a weeklong summer camp geared towards inner-city kids. The church even bought suitcases, new clothes and toiletries for the kids (most of them were unable to muster enough clothes or deodorant or soap for a week away). The night before their departure, we had each of the youth stay at a church member's home so as to ensure that the kids arrived at the camp bus on time with their luggage still packed and ready. We had two girls, aged thirteen or so, stay with us. In the morning, we became aware that our shampoo and some items from the guestroom were missing. We kindly asked the girls about the missing items, giving them the benefit of the doubt, but they denied any knowledge or culpability. During the car ride over to the church, we persisted in our requests for our things to no avail. When we arrived, we informed the camp chaperones of what had happened. They quizzed the girls and told them that if they did not return the items, they would not be allowed to go to camp. The girls refused to talk, and so their suitcases were unpacked. Out tumbled the pilfered items. The girls were sent home.

---

[12]Augustine *City of God* 11.15, trans. R. W. Dyson (New York: Cambridge University Press, 1998), p. 469.

Why did these girls do what they did? Why did they steal beauty products, especially when they had already been given a brand new set of shampoos and soaps by the church? Why did they jeopardize and finally lose their opportunity to attend a week-long youth camp for free? Why did they chose things that "pass away" instead of what "lives forever" (1 Jn 2:17)?

We might point toward social or economic factors, educational or developmental factors, racial or cultural factors. But in the end, there is no single explanatory reason. Sin is self-destructive. "The fall, in addition to causing the loss of original grace, shattered the equilibrium of human faculties. There is a kind of nemesis that follows sin and cannot fail to bear its fruits of devastation. . . . The state of sin, individual and social, original and actual, psychological and historical, is not a natural state but a *subnatural* one."[13]

On another occasion, my wife and I were laying on a blanket reading next to a little pond with ducks in it. We looked up and saw two boys, maybe eight or nine years old, chasing baby ducklings and slapping them upside the head with their shoes, which they had removed for the purpose. I could not believe my eyes. I jumped up and shooed the boys away. The good news is that none of the ducklings died, although a few had been knocked silly. Why would anyone do something so brutal and meaningless?

Sin is just like those two boys: cruel and senseless. What is more shocking is the ordinariness of such behavior.[14] As my personal anecdotes show, sin is mundane, it happens every day and involves everyone. It "so easily entangles" (Heb 12:1). Paul makes this point clear in Romans: "for we have already charged that all, both Jews and Greeks, are under the power of sin" (Rom 3:9 NRSV). Paul goes on in his open letter to the Romans to quote the Psalms:

> There is no one righteous, not even one;
>   there is no one who understands,

---

[13]Luigi Sturzo, *The True Life: Sociology of the Supernatural* (London: Geoffrey Bless, 1947), p. 29.

[14]See Hannah Arendt, *Eichmann in Jerusalem: A Report on the Banality of Evil* (New York: Penguin Classics, 1963).

no one who seeks God.
All have turned away,
   they have together become worthless;
   there is no one who does good,
   not even one. (Rom 3:10-12; Ps 14:1-3; 53:1-3)

The catastrophe takes the shape of a pandemic, a sickness affecting all. The plague introduced in Genesis 3, when the woman and her husband eat of a forbidden tree, spreads to their offspring as one brother, Cain, kills the other. Soon the whole earth is engulfed in wickedness, pride and revolt, as depicted in the story of Noah's flood and the tower of Babel. God's designs for relationship with humanity evaporate as the world spirals out of control.

ACT 3: COVENANT

At the point when all seems lost, the grand narrative of Genesis narrows down to the story of one family, that of Abram and his wife Sarai. Instead of attempting to reconcile the entire world at once, God attempts to build a relationship with one individual and through him and his family make peace with the world. As God makes a covenant with Abram, he tells him "and all the people on earth will be blessed through you" (Gen 12:3). The Lord vows to "make of you a great nation." He promises to bless Abram so that "you will be a blessing" (Gen 12:2). This new attempt at relationship with the descendents of Abram and Sarai will become a beacon of hope for others. God chooses to work through one family as a way of gathering up all the families of the earth. Augustine says the covenant concerns not only Abram's descendents, "but of all the nations that follow in the footsteps of his faith."[15]

God's call to Abram in Genesis 12 is truly one of the most remarkable moments in biblical history and in all of recorded history. "Now the LORD said to Abram, 'Go from your country and your kindred and your father's house to the land that I will show you.' . . . So, Abram went" (Gen 12:1, 4 NRSV). The covenant and call represent a radical shift from a cyclical view of history to a linear view. Throughout the

---

[15]Augustine *City of God* 16.16, p. 723.

Fertile Crescent of Abram's day, from Egypt to Canaan, Aram, Mesopotamia, Babylonia and the Sumer civilization, people held to a cyclical
view of time, which would have been a commonsensical view for pre-
literate, pre-scientific, agricultural cultures.

For the people of the Crescent, days cycled from dawn to noonday to
evening to night. The year was an unyielding progression, beginning
with spring, when new buds popped out of leafless tree limbs and
grasses pushed away soil. The farmer planted his seed. Animals began
to mate and reproduce. Spring gave way to summer, and the trees and
flowers and crops stretched to their full size. Then came autumn, when
the air began to cool, harvests were gathered and put away. And finally
the winter freezes reduced the landscape to a dormant barrenness. Even
so, spring was on its way to start the process over again. Life itself was
a grand circle, beginning with birth and proceeding to death. The infant arrived unable to communicate, dress, work or feed itself. As he or
she grew, these tasks and abilities were acquired until one reached the
full maturity of adulthood in full command of life and destiny. As old
age set in, bodily and mental functions began to decrease until the individual lost command of eating, dressing and communicating, and
succumbed to death. Life came full-circle, but not before the individual
reproduced and started the cycle of life again for the next generation.

The cults of the Fertile Crescent gave expression to this cyclical
rhythm, including worship of the sun and the moon, Baal, the Great
Wheel of Life and Death, the dying god Tammuz, and the fertility
gods of the Canaanites. There is great comfort in a cyclical view of life
and history: nothing ever changes, all things remain the same, there is
no need for risk or challenge or adventure. Friedrich Nietzsche darkly
described it as the eternal return of the same. Equal to the comfort of
repetition is the despair of sameness. Nothing ever changes and so there
is no hope of anything better. All dreams are washed out by the great
cycle in which everyone is trapped.

But here, in the heart of the Crescent, in Ur of the Chaldeans, God
commands Abram to go.

"See, I am doing a new thing" declares the Lord (Is 43:19). But who
is this God who speaks to Abram? Where did he come from? Does he

intend weal or woe? Abram does not know, and does not have the benefit of Scripture to find out. Where is this God leading him? The Lord responds, "to a land that I will show you." Abram's future is stamped with an enormous question mark, even if God has promised his protection and provision. For Abram the arrow of time points to the unknown future. Scholar Thomas Cahill comments that the words "Abram went" are

> two of the boldest words in all literature. They signal a complete depar-
> ture from everything that has gone before in the long evolution of cul-
> ture and sensibility. Out of Sumer, civilized repository of the predict-
> able, comes a man who does not know where he is going but goes forth
> into the unknown wilderness under the prompting of his god. Out of
> Mesopotamia, home of canny, self-serving merchants who use their
> gods to ensure prosperity and favor, comes a wealthy caravan with no
> material goal. Out of ancient humanity, which from the dim beginnings
> of its consciousness has read its eternal verities in the stars, comes a
> party traveling by no known compass. Out of the human race, which
> knows in its bones that all its striving must end in death, comes a leader
> who says he has been given an impossible promise. Out of mortal imag-
> ination comes a dream of something new, something better, something
> yet to happen, something—in the future.[16]

And, lest we fail to notice, the Genesis text reminds us that Abram was seventy-five years old when he received his calling to pick up and move. He was well past the age of adventure-taking just as his wife was well past the age of childbearing (Heb 11:11). Why did God call Abram when he was seventy-five, and not when he was twenty-five, at the height of his physical prowess? Why did this mysterious and unknown Lord wait until he should be settling into an easy retirement? At the end of the cycle when we should expect death, God brings life and new adventure. Our expectations are undermined and reversed. God starts not at the beginning but at the end. "See, the former things have taken place, and new things I declare" (Is 42:9).

Expectations are again reversed when God reveals to Abram in a

---

[16]Thomas Cahill, *The Gift of the Jews* (New York: Nan. A. Talese, 1998), p. 63.

vision what the sign of the covenant will be. God confirms to Abram that "you will be the father of many nations. No longer will you be called Abram; your name will be Abraham, for I have made you a father of many nations" (Gen 17:4-5). And likewise about his wife, Sarai, God says, "As for Sarai your wife, you are no longer to call her Sarai; her name will be Sarah. . . . I will bless her so that she will be the mother of nations; kings of peoples will come from her" (Gen 17:15-16). The irony is that Abram and Sarai—now Abraham ("father of a multitude") and Sarah ("princess")—do not have even one child between them, much less a multitude. And to boot, the text tells us that both husband and wife are well past the age of childbearing. This fact does not seem to deter God, who tells Abraham his part of the bargain:

> This is my covenant with you and your descendants after you, the covenant you are to keep: Every male among you shall be circumcised. You are to undergo circumcision, and it will be the sign of the covenant between me and you. (Gen 17:10-11)

The Latinized word for "covenant" is "testament" (as in the Old Testament and New Testament), which itself comes from *testis*.[17] The Latin word *testis* means "to testify" or "witness," but it can also refer to the male reproductive glands. Testimony and testicles share the same Latin root. Not only are they linguistically bound together, they are bound together in the Genesis text. The meaning of the text is clear, though unanticipated. God promises to make Abraham virile, Sarah fertile and their descendents numerous. At first this seems to sanction Abraham's place as the dominant male in a patriarchal society. Abraham will be the great father of his people. Feminist scholar Carol Delaney complains that because reproductivity is the essence of what God promises to Abraham, father Abraham's "penis [becomes] the holy place of

---

[17]The Latin word *testamentum* referred to "a will, publication of a will." It is an extension of *testari*, that is, "to make a will, be witness to," which is itself an extension of *testis*, "witness." The use of *testamentum* to indicate the two divisions of the Bible, vetus testamentum and novum testamentum, served in place of the Greek expressions *palaia diathēkē* and *kaine diathēkē*. The Greek word *diathēkē* carries both the sense of "covenant or dispensation" and "last will."

the covenant."[18] But any patriarchal peacocking is immediately under-cut by circumcision. It is not by Abraham's own virility and willpower that descendents will issue forth, it is by the plan and promise of God. The covenant is not a vindication of Abraham's virility. Instead, God demands that that skin be cut away from his member. The physical scar is forever a reminder that *God*, not male sexual potency or aggression, is the source of Abraham's descendents and Israel's strength. "So shall my covenant be in your flesh" (Gen 17:13 NRSV).

As the story of the covenant continues through the pages of the Hebrew Scriptures, Abraham's descendents do grow in number and in strength. The people become a nation with a law, language, culture, territory, military and so on. But eventually the nation splits in two. More disasters follow as the northern kingdom is destroyed by the Assyrians in the eighth century B.C. and the southern kingdom is destroyed by the Babylonians in the sixth century B.C. The remnant of Judah returns from exile in Babylon to a war-wrecked Jerusalem. Despair reigns. Hope drowns in tears. The question hanging like a dense fog at the conclusion of the Old Testament history is: Has the covenant exhausted itself? Has the story ended in failure? Has God abandoned the people?

Is there any sign of hope?

The post-exilic Jews begin to look to the prophets for any such sign. The prophets were those messengers from God who had a sense of the grand narrative. The prophets saw past the immediate situation. They saw that the epic of creation, catastrophe and covenant would not end in tragedy, but would somehow be consummated in victory.

> "The time is coming," declares the LORD,
>   "when I will make a new covenant
>   with the house of Israel
>   and with the house of Judah.
> It will not be like the covenant
>   I made with their forefathers
>   when I took them by the hand

---

[18]Carol Delaney, "The Legacy of Abraham," *Anti-Covenant: Counter-Reading Women's Lives in the Hebrew Bible*, ed. Mieke Bal (Decatur, Ga.: Almond Press, 1989), p. 35.

to lead them out of Egypt,
because they broke my covenant,
though I was a husband to them,"
declares the LORD.
"This is the covenant I will make with the house of Israel
after that time," declares the LORD.
"I will put my law in their minds
and write it on their hearts.
I will be their God,
and they will be my people." (Jer 31:31-33)

The Lord was preparing a new covenant unlike the old covenant for
the people, a covenant written not upon tablets of stone, but upon the
heart. How would this new covenant be recognized? Who would bear
it to the people?

"The days are coming," declares the LORD, "when I will fulfill the gra-
cious promise I made to the house of Israel and to the house of Judah.
"In those days and at that time
I will make a righteous Branch sprout from David's line;
he will do what is just and right in the land." (Jer 33:14-15)

As the rabbis and scribes scanned the texts for signs of a new hope,
they homed in on this "righteous Branch," this "son of David." This was
the hero they were hoping for; one who would stand up for the people,
liberate Israel from the Romans and inaugurate a new day. This figure
would be the anointed one of the LORD—in Hebrew "the anointed
one" is *Messiah* and in Greek it is *Christ*.

With this background, we are now in a position to consider the story
told in Luke 4, where Jesus is invited to read a passage of Scripture at
his hometown synagogue in Nazareth. Many youngsters have been invited by their pastors to do the same thing. Jesus stood up, unrolled the
scroll to Isaiah.

The Spirit of the Sovereign LORD is on me,
because the LORD has anointed me
to preach good news to the poor.
He has sent me to bind up the brokenhearted,

> to proclaim freedom for the captives
> and release from darkness for the prisoners,
> to proclaim the year of the LORD's favor. (Is 61:1)

Then he rolled the scroll back up, handed it to the attendant and said, "Today this scripture is fulfilled in your hearing" (Lk 4:21). What could this mean? At first the congregation at Nazareth was dazed by his comment. But as Jesus continued to talk, the people's confusion hardened into rage. The text from Isaiah is about the Lord's Anointed One, the Messiah, the Christ. The son of Joseph, a local boy, could not be the Anointed One; Jesus didn't know what he was saying. As everyone understood, the Messiah would ride in on a white stallion, his sword gleaming and his army ready for war.

Members of the synagogue leapt to their feet, grabbed Jesus and threw him out of town. Jesus had touched on a raw nerve. The messianic expectations of the people were not to be trifled with. Jesus had tapped into the deepest fears and hopes of the Jewish people.

Part of Jesus' task, then, would be to redefine Messiah for a people who were right about their need for a savior, but wrong about what needed saving. It was all there in the Prophets, but the people had not appreciated the full witness of the Prophets. Indeed, a few chapters prior to the triumphant declarations of Isaiah 61 read by Jesus, one finds other words about this Anointed One that are not so reassuring. They are, in fact, quite distressing.

> Surely he took up our infirmities
> and carried our sorrows,
> yet we considered him stricken by God,
> smitten by him, and afflicted.
> But he was pierced for our transgressions,
> he was crushed for our iniquities;
> the punishment that brought us peace was upon him,
> and by his wounds we are healed.
> We all, like sheep, have gone astray,
> each of us has turned to his own way;
> and the LORD has laid on him
> the iniquity of us all. (Is 53:4-6)

The triumphant Messiah was also to be the suffering servant. The Son of God was no more than a son of man. The Christ had not come to kill for his people but to die for his people. "For the Son of Man came not to be served but to serve, and to give his life as a ransom for many" (Mk 10:45). This was the reversal to end all reversals. The messianic expectations of many were shattered in a thousand pieces. No wonder the congregation at Nazareth hurled Jesus out of town.

The story takes a drastic and unexpected turn. The Creator has entered the creation not to flood the earth or destroy the wicked with brimstone, but to die for what he made—upon him is the punishment that makes us whole.

4

CHRISTIANITY AS STORY

RECONCILIATION

ACT 4: CHRIST

IN THE FOURTH ACT OF THE DRAMA, we reach the climactic moment of truth. When all seems lost, God, the author of the story, steps into his own story . . . and speaks a Word. What is this Word, unleashed from eternity, flinging stars across the sky, bringing worlds into being and reverberating so loudly that even the stones cry out (Lk 19:40)? What message does God speak to a world spinning off its axis? What does God say? As Scripture tells us, God does not say some-*thing*—but some*one*, a name: Jesus. The astonishing claim of Christianity is that the very Word of the originator and sustainer of the universe was born, lived, breathed and "made his dwelling among us. We have seen his glory, the glory of the One and Only, who came from the Father, full of grace and truth" (Jn 1:14).

The God who reigns in eternity, whose wisdom and authority are infinite, whose life will have no end, this same God becomes finite, limited, weak, the child of Mary, born in a Bethlehem stable. God writ large is now writ small. The author becomes a character in his own story. The divine story is identified with our story in the person of Jesus.

Incarnation. The story of creation, catastrophe and covenant culminates in the womb of one young mother-to-be, Mary, betrothed to Joseph. "Therefore Israel will be abandoned until the time when she who is in labor gives birth" (Mic 5:3). The twelfth-century abbess of the convent at Rupertsberg, Hildegard von Bingen, extols Mary's role in the drama, "More than all that Eve lost is the blessing you won. . . . May the limbs of your son be the chords of the song the angels chant above."[1] Mary, who is overshadowed by the Spirit, gives birth to the savior, the Messiah, the new covenant in the flesh. Whereas the old covenant was marked by the removal of flesh in circumcision, the new covenant puts on flesh in the incarnation.

The relationship between Creator and creation that had been fractured in the Fall and re-established in the Abrahamic covenant comes together now in this one baby born of Mary in an animal stall in Bethlehem. Irenaeus of Lyons (c. 125–c. 202) wonders in amazement, "What new thing did the Lord bring by coming down to earth?"[2] Although Irenaeus originally haled from the eastern end of Asia Minor, he was sent as a missionary to a fledgling Christian community in the wild-west boomtown of Lyons, located in the Rhône-Alpes of Gaul. Despite being cut off from his intellectual and spiritual roots, he thought deeply and wrote profoundly about the character of Christ and the role he plays in the Christian drama. Irenaeus sees a point of comparison between Jesus and the Old Testament ark of the covenant. As the ark contained the tablets of stone on which the old covenant was etched, so Jesus contains the new covenant to be etched upon our hearts. And, "as the ark was gilded within and without with pure gold, so was also the body of Christ pure and resplendent; for it was adorned within by the Word, and shielded without by the Spirit."[3] Inside the ark was placed the staff of Aaron, a bowl of manna and the tablets of the Law; in the incarnation we encounter the new staff of God, the new bread of life and the new law of the Spirit. The story of creation and covenant has come full circle in Jesus the Christ, "the mediator of a new covenant" (Heb 12:24). Creator and creation unite in one person; the relationship is restored in one man who will in turn restore all "by a new and living way opened for us through the curtain, that is, his body" (Heb 10:20).[4]

---

[1]Hildegard von Bingen, "O virga ac diadema," *Voices of Angels: Music of Hildegard von Bingen* (Hollywood: Delos International, 1997), musical recording.
[2]Irenaeus *Against the Heresies* 4.34.1, ANF, vol. 1, p. 511.
[3]Irenaeus "Fragment" 8, ANF, vol. 1, p. 570.
[4]British theologian John Milbank observes, "Christ is the unexpected fulfillment of human

Thomas Cahill brings to our attention the Roman Martyrology, a sprawling calendrical record of Christian martyrs that became popular during the Middle Ages. The Martyrology calendar has no single author, but each generation that inherited it added to it before passing it on. The majestic entry for the twenty-fifth day of December cascades down the page:

> In the 5199th year since the creation of the world,
> when in the beginning God made heaven and earth;
> the 2957th year since the Flood;
> the 2015th year since the birth of Abraham;
> the 1510th year since Moses
> and the going forth of the People of Israel from Egypt;
> the 1032nd year since David's royal anointing;
> in the 65th week, according to the Prophecy of Daniel;
> in the 194th Olympiad;
> the 752nd year from the Foundation of the City of Rome;
> the 42nd year of the Rule of Octavian Augustus, all the world
>   being at peace,
> in the sixth age of the world,
> JESUS CHRIST,
> eternal God and Son of the eternal Father,
> desiring to sanctify the world by his most merciful coming,
> being conceived by the Holy Spirit,
> and nine months having passed since his conception,
> IN BETHLEHEM OF JUDEA WAS BORN,
> OF THE VIRGIN MARY MADE MAN –
> the Birthday of our Lord Jesus Christ according to the flesh.[5]

To this we can only add a hearty amen! He is born! Jesus is the central character of the biblical story and of history itself. The Hebrew and Greek Scriptures act as two compass needles and Jesus as the magnetic center. The Hebrew Scriptures point inexorably towards him and the Greek Scriptures likewise lead back to him. Or, to use a mathematical

---

intent, the proper word for God, and the true fulfillment of Creation in the realm of human works" (Milbank, *The Word Made Strange* [New York: Blackwell, 1997], p. 139).

[5]Quoted in Thomas Cahill, *Mysteries of the Middle Ages* (New York: Nan A. Talese, 2006), pp. 51-52.

analogy, Scripture is the sequence of numbers (5, 10, 15, 20 . . .) and Christ is the formula (5 x N, where N = 1, 2, 3, 4 . . .).[6] Or, to change the analogy again, Jesus is the magnifying glass under which the pages of Scripture are to be viewed.

Since Jesus is the most important character in Scripture and indeed the heart of the Christian faith, one would think that Scripture would speak of Jesus in very clear and precise terms. We might expect Scripture to give a very exact definition of Jesus' identity. Contrary to expectations, the New Testament does not do this but swamps the reader with images, titles and metaphors: Jesus is the Bread (Jn 6:41), the Deliverer (Rom 11:26), the second Adam (1 Cor 15:45), the Image of God (2 Cor 4:4), the Cornerstone (Eph 2:20), the Alpha and the Omega (Rev 1:8). He is the King (Mt 21:5) and the Servant (Mt 12:18), the eternal Word of God (Jn 1:1) and the Firstborn of the dead (Rev 1:5), the Son of God (Lk 4:41) and the Son of Man (Mk 8:31), the Lamb that was sacrificially slain (Rev 5:12) and the Priest who forever makes sacrifice (Heb 5:6). Christians—faithful to the witness of Scripture—must be careful not to pick and choose which of these images we like best and which we do not. Nor can this cornucopia of images be reduced down to a single essential point of representation. Christ splendors in all of these images and titles; more than that, he absorbs every scriptural character and event and revelation in himself in a way that unsettles and fulfills, breaks and heals, dissolves and preserves.

Christ is Lord of earth and heaven *and* Scripture. "As through being a faithful son of Israel Jesus is Israel's King of Kings, so through perfect obedience to [the Scriptures] Jesus is Scripture's ultimate authority." Westmont College professor Telford Work declares, "In obeying and fulfilling Scripture, he is revealed to be more than its servant. He is the very Lord *of* Scripture."[7] The most proper response to such a Lord is to fall down in worship and sing with the chorus of angels surrounding the throne in Revelation,

---

[6]John O'Keefe and R. R. Reno, *Sanctified Vision* (Baltimore, Md.: Johns Hopkins University Press, 2005), p. 39.
[7]Telford Work, *Living and Active: Scripture in the Economy of Salvation* (Grand Rapids: Eerdmans, 2002), p. 172.

Worthy is the Lamb, who was slain,
to receive power and wealth and wisdom and strength
and honor and glory and praise! (Rev 5:12)

There is endless beauty and complexity in the scriptural witness to this Lord of lords. The Jesus we find in Scripture might be compared to a crystal in the window of God's glory, reflecting and refracting light in endless directions. Origen (c. 185–254) called the Son the "stainless mirror" of the Father.[8] The truth is that when we encounter Christ, the end result is not a tidy explanation of a certain historical personality but a change in us—we are healed, we surrender in worship, we are made new. The treasure box of pictures contained in Scripture help us find ways to express and articulate this great effect.

Historicity. One particularly cumbersome question that cannot be dodged in our day and age is the question of historicity. Did Jesus of Nazareth really exist in the way Scripture reports? Can we trust that the four Gospels have given us an accurate and exact representation of Jesus? Did he do all that the Gospels say he did? Are any of the stories and sayings perhaps legendary? Although it breaks the flow of the narrative, we must pause to consider some of these questions and to establish the grounds for trusting the historicity of the Gospel stories.

Even the believer who dismisses out of hand any questioning of the Gospel writers' integrity must at some point acknowledge the obvious differences between the four Gospels. Compare the Sermon on the Mount in Matthew 5–7 with the Sermon on the Plain in Luke 6; the timing of the clearing of the temple in John 2 with Matthew 21, Mark 11 and Luke 19; or the feeding of the five thousand story told in Matthew 14, Mark 6, Luke 9 and John 6; or the last words of Jesus before he expired on the cross, as found in Mark 15, Luke 23 and John 19.[9] You will find variations in wording, actions and order of events, some of which are minor and others more significant.

Scholars have spent careers accounting for these differences. To some readers, these variations between the Gospels are especially jar-

---

[8]Origen *De Principiis* 1.2, ANF, vol. 4, p. 248.

[9]Try Bart Ehrman's experiment on the four Gospel accounts of the resurrection. *Peter, Paul, and Mary Magdalene* (New York: Oxford University Press, 2006), pp. 227-29.

ring. Either Jesus said something or he did not say something. Either he said it this way or he said it that way. Textual discrepancies turn into full-blown contradictions that undermine the authenticity and authority of the account. We need not take such an extreme view. I would argue that textual variations do not undermine the authenticity of the stories, but actually bolster it. We have not *one* witness to the actions and words of Jesus, but several independent witnesses. The junior high principal who wants to find out how a hallway fight started does not ask just one eyewitness, but multiple eyewitnesses, whose accounts vary with their individual perspective. It is not that one is right and the others are wrong; the multiple testimonies create a composite picture that is truthful and real *because* of its different perspectives.

The point is that the "real" and "historical" Jesus is *testified* to by the four Gospel writers in their own and independent ways. Richard Bauckham, in his thoroughly researched and masterfully documented study of *Jesus and the Eyewitnesses*, demonstrates compellingly the historical reliability of the Gospel stories as records of eyewitness reports.[10] The key to appreciating Gospel's historical reliability is in appreciating the fact that they are testimonies from eyewitnesses. As Bauckham points out, it is not that the Gospels give us personal testimony *instead* of history; it is rather that the kind of historiography that the Gospel writers engage in is *testimony*. There are many ways of conducting history—statistical data-collection, archaeology or archival research—and the way that the Gospels conduct it is through eyewitness reporting. Practically speaking, this means that the independence of the four accounts should not be tampered with, lest the testimony be sullied. Our

---

[10]Richard Bauckham, *Jesus and the Eyewitnesses* (Grand Rapids: Eerdmans, 2006), pp. 5-8. "As a form of historiography testimony offers a unique access to historical reality that cannot be had without an element of trust in the credibility of the witness and what he or she has to report. Testimony is irreducible; we cannot, at least in some of its most distinctive and valuable claims, go behind it and make our own autonomous verification of them; we cannot establish the truth of testimony for ourselves as though we stood where the witnesses uniquely stood. Eyewitness testimony offers us insider knowledge from involved participants. It also offers us engaged interpretation, for in testimony fact and meaning coinhere, and witnesses who give testimony do so with the conviction of significance that requires to be told" (p. 505). For this reason, Bauckham argues that "testimony" offers not only a historiographic category, but a theological one. It is theologically significant that the Gospels, as revelation, are presented as eyewitness testimony—for revelation is personal disclosure of God to humans.

tendency is to want to smooth out all the ruffles and disagreements between Matthew, Mark, Luke and John. In A.D. 423, bishop Theodoret of Cyrrhus had copies of Tatian's *Diatessaron* seized and burned because in that work Tatian had compiled and consolidated the stories of the four Gospels into a single narrative. What did Theodoret find so objectionable? What was wrong with harmonizing the four Gospels? Theodoret felt it essential to preserve the diversity of the four witnesses.[11] Although we might disagree with his solution to the problem, we can respect Theodoret's intention. Harmony at the expense of honesty does not produce worthwhile dividends.

Many Christians get the impression that Matthew, Mark, Luke and John were put in the New Testament because they were the sole surviving records of Jesus' life left to the church. The church fathers just included everything they had. But scholars are becoming increasingly aware that this was most definitely not the case. The early church had a vast array of gospels from which to choose. A number of other ancient "gospels" were available to them, like The Infancy Gospel of Thomas, The Secret Gospel of Mark, The Gospel of the Egyptians, The Gospel of Truth, The Gospel of the Ebionites and so on.[12] Were these not also eyewitness testimonies? Many of these simply repeat or summarize teachings and events recorded in the canonical Gospels. Others of them add new sayings, events and miracles. What should be done with these writings?

Contrary to what Dan Brown would have us believe, there was no conspiracy in the early church to suppress "the real story" of Jesus as told by these "other gospels." Instead, the broad consensus of the church was to reject them from inclusion into the Christian canon for very legitimate reasons: they contained unverified, distorted or legendary accounts of Jesus or because they used the stories of Jesus to promote

---

[11]William Placher, *Narratives of a Vulnerable God* (Louisville: Westminster John Knox, 1994), p. 87.

[12]Many of the known "gospels" that did not make it into the canon have been collected into a single volume, *Lost Scriptures*, ed. Bart Ehrman (New York: Oxford University Press, 2003). For the recently published Gospel of Judas, see Elaine Pagels and Karen King, *Reading Judas: The Gospel of Judas and the Shaping of Christianity* (New York: Penguin, 2008). For a well-balanced and fair introduction to these alternative gospels and their contexts, see Elaine Pagels, *The Gnostic Gospels* (New York: Random House, 1979), and Elaine Pagels, *Beyond Belief* (New York: Vintage, 2004).

Gnostic dissension in the church. For instance, The Infancy Gospel of Thomas tells of the boy Jesus shaping clay birds and breathing life into them, zapping a neighborhood bully with the death curse and generally acting strange. I encourage believers to go to their libraries and read the Nag Hammadi codices that contain these "other gospels." They will quickly discover for themselves why these writings were excluded from the canon of the New Testament. The church fathers, under the guidance of the Holy Spirit, scrutinized and tested the Gospels thoroughly before including them in the canon. Matthew, Mark, Luke and John, more than any others, bore true witness to the Word made flesh.

Death. One question looms large over Jesus' ministry on earth, as recorded by all four New Testament Gospels: the question of identity. Who was this man from Nazareth? A rabbi? A king? A revolutionary? A carpenter's son? God's Son? Some received him as the possible Messiah, the long-awaited hero come to liberate the Jews from Roman occupation, just as Judas Maccabeus "The Hammer" had done two hundred years earlier when the Jews were under the thumb of the Seleucids. Others saw Jesus of Nazareth as a pretender Messiah come to stir up trouble. Jesus himself addressed some of the misguided expectations. He said, in so many words, that if people were going to use the word "Messiah" of him, they must use it in a totally different way. He pushed his listeners to reimagine what kind of hero they really needed, and what kind of saving they really needed.

He came to tell a new story, or rather, an old story in a new way. It was a tale of a covenant and a kingdom that for once did not end with a military confrontation, but with peace and forgiveness. It was not an easy story to hear. The responses to his retelling of the story were predictable: misunderstanding, fear, disappointment and anger. Ultimately, his new narrative is too much to handle. Jesus must be done away with and put to death.

Flavius Josephus (c. 37–100) lived an extraordinary life in extraordinary times; trained as a priest but pressed into military service as a young man, he was given command of the Jewish defense forces with the task of halting nothing less than the Roman army. The Roman military machine laid siege to him at Jotapata. An estimated 40,000 died, but not Josephus. He survived only to be captured. He was handed over to Vespasian, who took him to Rome where he won the patronage of the imperial household, eventually becoming a Roman citizen. As a result of winning the favor of the emperor, he was granted the time and provisions to sit down and record for posterity's sake the history of the Jewish revolt against Rome. The result was his *Jewish Wars.*

The *Jewish Wars* is not a happy story. It is replete with bloody sieges, skirmishes, reprisals, infighting and treachery, all leading up to the shocking destruction of Jerusalem in the year A.D. 70. Even though some scholars suspect that Josephus exaggerates the number of deaths, it is nonetheless clear from his account that Judea and Galilee were not safe places in the first century. Violent factions of Jews seized local towns and forts as garrisons against the Romans, expelling or putting to death Jews who sympathized with the Romans or refused to get involved. Roman procurators and commanders unmercifully slaughtered the people of the land, many times regardless of whether they were associated with the insurrectionists. The fomented fury of the first century would eventually leave thousands upon thousands of Jews dislocated or dead.

So, the fact that *one* Jew, a man named Jesus, was put to death during those helter-skelter days by Roman crucifixion under the suspicion of sedition—is in itself not an astounding fact or a stretch of the imagination. One gets the impression from Josephus that this was nearly an everyday occurrence. And yet, the followers of Jesus staked their lives on the claim that this death was different. There was more to the story.

The death of this man was unique. The four Gospels devote much more time to the trial and crucifixion of Jesus than to any other episode in his life, showing us how important this one episode is to the whole plot. The Gospels turn on the death. Yet, something is not quite right. Despite their care and attention to the what, where, how and who of the story, the Gospel writers nonetheless "present us with a very confusing and complex account."[13]

Jesus returned, against all warnings, to Jerusalem for Passover celebrations.[14] His whereabouts were "betrayed" by Judas, one of his own,

---

[13]John Milbank, *Being Reconciled* (New York: Routledge, 2003), p. 81.
[14]I will not cite specific verses here. For the full account see Mk 14–15; Mt 26–27; Lk 22–23; Jn 18–19.

to the local Sanhedrin. It is a strange betrayal since Jesus had made no effort to hide from his opponents. He understood full well that "the Son of Man will be handed over to be crucified" (Mt 26:2). He was seized by an amorphous gang of armed men and delivered in the darkness of night to Caiaphas at an impromptu meeting of the Sanhedrin, the local Jewish assembly.[15]

As light dawned on that infamous Friday, Jesus was bound and brought to Pilate, the Roman procurator empowered to issue death sentences. Jesus stood accused of perverting the people and declaring himself to be King of the Jews in rivalry to Caesar. Luke records that Pilate attempted to pawn the problem off on Herod, but that Herod sent him back without satisfying the request for a death sentence. By now a sizeable crowd had gathered. Pilate offered as a compromise the release of either Barabbas or Jesus; the agitated mob cries out for the release of Barabbas, an insurrectionist, and the crucifixion of Jesus, presumably also an insurrectionist. Pilate consented, but his behavior is contradictory. He washed his hands of the business, finding no fault in Jesus, but permitting Roman soldiers to do the will of the people and execute the man. Pilate both condemns and acquits Jesus. All four Gospels agree, he "handed him over to be crucified" (Mt 27:26; Mk 15:15; Lk 23:25; Jn 19:16).

In fact, throughout the narrative Jesus is again and again *handed over* from one group to another. John Milbank asks,

> Who then really killed Jesus and why? And why did Jesus submit to this? The only consistent thread in these narratives is that Christ was constantly handed over, or abandoned to another party. Judas betrayed his presence; the disciples deserted him; the Sanhedrin gave him up to Pilate; Pilate in turn to Herod; Herod back to Pilate; Pilate again to the mob who finally gave him over to a Roman execution, which somehow, improperly, they co-opted. Even in his death, Jesus was still being handed back and forth, as if no one actually killed him, but he died from neglect and lack of his own living space.[16]

Who killed Jesus? The most immediate answer is the Roman centu-

---

[15]John actually says he was taken to Annas first, and then to Caiaphas (Jn 18:12-14).
[16]Milbank, *Being Reconciled*, p. 82.

rions who actually nailed his feet and hands to the cross. But of course, they were acting not on their own accord; they acted on the orders of Pilate—except that Pilate washed his hands of the whole thing. We might blame the mob, the restless crowd of people who called for Jesus' blood. But aren't these the same people who had welcomed Jesus at the beginning of the week with palm branches? Mobs are fickle. The Sanhedrin was responsible for whipping up the onlookers and charging Jesus. So, maybe we should blame the Sanhedrin. The problem is, not everyone on the Sanhedrin agreed with what the council was doing. And, in point of fact, the Sanhedrin did not have the authority to carry out an execution. None of them actually did the deed. Someone else did. Theologically speaking, we affirm that we are *all* responsible for the death of Jesus, "who was handed over to death for *our* trespasses" (Rom 4:25 NRSV, emphasis mine). But I wasn't there, and neither were you. None of us drove the nails; none of us demanded his death.

Perhaps God himself is responsible for allowing it to happen. Peter points his finger at the Pentecostal crowds in Jerusalem and exclaims, "This man was handed over to you *by God's set purpose* and foreknowledge" (Acts 2:23, emphasis mine). As the prophet Jeremiah said, "He has handed me over to those I cannot withstand" (Jer 1:14). And yet, even if we concede that God permitted the event, we cannot say God killed his Son. Everyone made their own choices.

We are ashamed to admit that, for the most part, Jesus' death is an embarrassment. When pressed, we cannot give a good reason why he was put to death; we cannot even say who should be held responsible for putting him to death. It all seems so muddled, and it makes Jesus seem so weak. We would much prefer the gospel of the Saxons, the *Heliand*, written in the ninth century in order to promote Christian faith among those "perfidious" Saxon tribes. The *Heliand* depicts Jesus as a Saxon liege lord and the apostles as his fierce defenders and loyal thanes. When Peter strikes off the ear of Malchus, the *Heliand* says,

> Then wrathful and raging
> The fearless fighter stepped to the front,
> Near to his prince, his noble lord.
> His heart beat high; undaunted he drew

His sword from his side and struck with full might
At the foremost foe, so that Malchus was maimed
By the sharp-edged blade. He struck off his ear,
Slashing the head, slitting the cheek.
Bright from the gash bubbled the blood,
Welling from the wound.[17]

The *Heliand* is a hot-blooded action gospel for warriors, not cowards. No weakness or indecision here. This is the kind of gospel we would like! This is the kind of Jesus we could respect.

Contrary to what we would prefer, the New Testament story tolls cacophony and dissonance. It staggers between innocence and guilt, the macabre and the tragic, light and dark, confusion and betrayal; "the killing of Jesus is the ultimate contrast between the nonviolent reign of God and the rule of evil."[18]

A plot in free-fall. The furrow-browed Paul of Tarsus, veteran missionary and evangelist of the Mediterranean, warns against over-adorning the Christian message "with words of human wisdom, lest the cross be emptied of its power" (1 Cor 1:17). He states bluntly, "we preach Christ crucified" (1 Cor 1:23). Nothing more, nothing less. "May I never boast except in the cross of our Lord Jesus Christ" (Gal 6:14). "The nucleus of everything that Christian theology says about 'God'" declares the contemporary German theologian Jürgen Moltmann, "is to be found in this Christ event. The Christ event on the cross is a God event."[19] This is, as Athanasius says, the "monument of victory," the capstone to top it all, the arch of triumph under which the victorious church passes in parade.[20]

Artistic depictions of Christ on the cross are hard to find before the year 400. One of the earliest, maybe as early as A.D. 400, is the ivory

---

[17]See Richard Winston, *Charlemagne: From the Hammer to the Cross* (Indianapolis: Bobbs-Merrill, 1954), p. 64.

[18]J. Denny Weaver, "Violence in Christian Theology," in *Cross Examinations: Readings on the Meaning of the Cross Today*, ed. Marit Trelstad (Minneapolis: Augsburg Fortress, 2006), p. 239.

[19]Jürgen Moltmann, *The Crucified God*, trans. R. Wilson and J. Bowden (Minneapolis: Fortress, 1993), p. 205.

[20]Athanasius *On the Incarnation* 19 (Crestwood, N.Y.: St. Vladimir's Seminary Press, 2000), p. 48.

carving pictured above, which is now housed in the British Museum.

The Yale historian Roland Bainton offers this description of the carved scene:

> The title above the head of Christ, *Rex Jud.*, is Latin for "King of the Jews." Christ is alive. His eyes are open. The arms are horizontal; the body, vertical. The feet appear to have no support. The chin is beardless. There is no halo. The two figures on the left are Mary and John. The figure on the other side may be a soldier who pierced Christ's body, though he appears to be about to strike a blow. On the far left, Judas is hanging himself. The thirty pieces of silver spill out at his feet. On a branch of the tree above a dove is feeding her fledglings.[21]

This plaque, most likely one of four that would have been mounted to the four sides of a small casket, juxtaposes Christ's submission to death with Judas's suicide. Judas is driven by despair and shame to com-

---

[21]Roland Bainton, *Behold the Christ* (New York: Harper & Row, 1974), p. 146. One correction to professor Bainton's description is that there is a halo etched into the ivory behind his head. It is not protruding, but you can see its outline.

mit a rash and heinous act of suicide. Jesus accepts his death willingly, making it an act of purpose and sacrifice. Notice the eyes—while Judas's eyes are closed and his head is twisted back, Christ fixes his eyes forward, upon us, as if to answer our questioning glances, "Yes." He is King of kings and Lord of lords. His act of surrender is for *us* and our salvation. His victory over the powers of death extends to those under the shadow of his outstretched arms, to the Roman on the right as well as his disciple and mother on the left. It extends unto Judas himself and, if we are willing, unto us who meet his gaze.

The force of the cross knocks us off balance. We cannot account for its dizzying effect on us by recourse to psychological, sociological or anthropological explanations. Human rationalizations simply do not suffice to explain the power of the gospel: Christ Jesus, beloved and chosen by God from before the foundation of the world, is bruised for our iniquities, beaten for our infirmities, brought low so that we might be lifted up. Irenaeus, who personally witnessed the fragility of life in the hot summer of 177 when Christians in his hometown of Lyons were rounded up en masse and publicly slaughtered at a patriotic festival, says, "He who was then in heaven . . . descended into the dust of death."[22]

Through the weakness of the cross and the cruelty of its punishment, God saves men and women. But *how*, exactly? What does it mean to say that God saves us through the death of Jesus? How does the Son of God's death forgive sins? How does this one death change anything? These are deep, important and mystery-laden questions. And, by God's good grace, the New Testament does not lack answers. It bursts at the seams with metaphors and comparisons and descriptions and explanations. The cross, as a completely unique, novel and unrepeatable event, as a display of profound divine revelation, as the turning-point of history itself, affecting all of humanity, cannot be condensed and contained in just one explanation. Instead, we encounter dozens.

The cross represents the victory of God over the power of death and the devil. The author of Hebrews says,

---

[22]Irenaeus *Against Heresies* 4.19, ANF, vol. 1, p. 490.

> But we see Jesus, who was made a little lower than the angels, now crowned with glory and honor because he suffered death, so that by the grace of God he might taste death for everyone. . . . he too shared in their humanity so that by his death he might destroy him who holds the power of death—that is, the devil. (Heb 2:9-10, 14)

Not only was it a victory, the cross was God's way of buying back humanity from sin and shame, at the cost of Christ's own blood. In 1 Peter we read, "For you know that it was not with perishable things such as silver or gold that you were redeemed from the empty way of life handed down to you from your forefathers, but with the precious blood of Christ, a lamb without blemish or defect" (1 Pet 1:18-19). Christ was the "Lamb of God" sent as a pure and innocent sacrifice for sin, as Isaiah 53 laments, "like a lamb to the slaughter . . . the LORD makes his life a guilt offering" (Is 53:7, 10). Indeed, Isaiah 53, where the suffering and sacrifice of the Servant of God is most vividly depicted, is referenced in Romans 4:25; 5:18-19; 1 Corinthians 15:3; 2 Corinthians 5:21; Galatians 4:27; Philippians 2:9-11; Hebrews 5:8; 9:28; and 1 Peter 2:22-25. As can be observed from this spread, the New Testament authors clearly understood Jesus' death as the sacrifice Isaiah foretold. More to the point, his death put and *end* to sacrifice (Heb 9–10). Not only was Christ the final sacrifice, he was "born of a woman, born under law, to redeem those under law" (Gal 4:4-5). Christ accepted the legal penalty for humanity's misdeeds so that he might liberate us from the law and its demands: "Christ redeemed us from the curse of the law by becoming a curse for us" (Gal 3:13).

These verses are but a small sample of the vast array of images in the Bible depicting and describing the cross and its meaning. And, by the way, the images are not mutually exclusive. There are no strict divisions between where one metaphor starts and another ends. In the New Testament, judicial, sacrificial, familial and military metaphors often splash against one another—juxtaposing, contrasting, supporting and enriching. Baptist theologian James McClendon takes the first chapter of Colossians as a perfect example, where legal and sacrificial images swirl with those of slave-redemption:

A rash of metaphors of the cross break forth in this text. The cross is rescue and release—here are metaphors of family-redemption (1:13). The cross is reconciliation (*apokatēllaxen*, 1:21) a term that simply means to change or make change—for example to settle a commercial account. The shameful "death in his body of flesh and blood" (no metaphor, but grisly fact) "reconciles" by bringing disciples into God's presence. The word used for presence (*parastēsai*, 1:22) is frequently a legal term, as when a court requires one in custody to be *presented* for judgment. At this judgment, though, believers are presented "without blame or blemish" (1:22)—a sacrificial image.[23]

McClendon shows that each image takes root and sprouts "without cost to the overall intention of the author to show the story of the cross beyond every metaphor, human shame turned into God's grace."[24] We should not fixate on any one image to the exclusion of the others. We must keep sight of the main plot.

God in Christ died for our sins, not because God had to, but because God chose to. "We are the spared because God refuses to have us lost."[25] This is the tale of a God who so loved the work of his hand he bled for it. Into the hands of the Father the Son concedes his Spirit—and it is there that the length and depth and breadth of God's love is displayed (Lk 23:43).

Sin and guilt drive us to despair and abandonment; the Father's love in his Son on the cross chases and catches that which has been abandoned and despaired. God loves in freedom; freely God sends his Son and freely the Son lays down his life out of love for us, "while we were still sinners" (Rom 5:8) no less! This is the work of God, streaking down from the black sky like lightning and exploding with a bang heard around the world. Everything hinges on the death of God's Son. This is the moment after which there is no future; this is the edge beyond which there is nothing; this is the death of God, the end of everything.

---

[23]James McClendon Jr., *Systematic Theology II: Doctrine* (Nashville: Abingdon, 1994), p. 227.
[24]Ibid.
[25]Stanley Hauerwas, *Cross-Shattered Christ* (Grand Rapids: Brazos, 2004), p. 66.

5

CHRISTIANITY AS STORY

ENDINGS AND BEGINNINGS

RESURRECTION

AND THE END CAME. "He has appeared once for all at the end of the ages to do away with sin by the sacrifice of himself" (Heb 9:26). Jesus died. Like a lamb led to the slaughter, he was taken to his death. He was laid in the tomb a cold, pale, lifeless body. All went silent. All went gray. Death is the end of things, the final word.

Or is it?

Here our story jumps its track. "But God raised him from the dead, freeing him from the agony of death" (Acts 2:24). Death does not have the last word. There is yet one more word to be heard. The primordial pattern of birth, life and death is broken; after death comes rebirth, new life, resurrection. "He was not abandoned to the grave, nor did his body see decay" (Acts 2:31). Sunrise exchanges horizons with sunset. On the third day of entombment, the stone was discovered rolled away from the tomb and the corpse inside missing—a divine suspension of *habeas corpus*. The angel announces to the alarmed women who arrive at the tomb, "He has risen; he is not here. See the place where they laid him" (Mk 16:6). As if with eyebrows raised, William Cavanaugh remarks, "Christianity itself is founded on a disappearance. The tomb is empty, the body is gone."[1]

The resurrected Jesus, though absent from the tomb, presents him-

---

[1]William Cavanaugh, *Torture and Eucharist* (Malden, Mass.: Blackwell, 1998), p. 281.

self elsewhere. He appears to the disciples and many others, we are told, during a strange forty-day period following the resurrection. What is the resurrected Lord like? What kind of body does he possess? By all accounts, he has a physical body like us: he eats a breakfast of fish with his close friends, invites Thomas to touch him and is recognized by his followers as the same Jesus born in Bethlehem they once knew. This is no ghost or angelic being. This really is Jesus—but something is different. He is uncocooned. He still bears the open wounds of his death, which presumably should still be killing him, but are not. His injuries are healed without being stitched up—the resurrected one is *still* the crucified one. He appears and disappears at will, even through locked doors. His relation to space and locality has changed. Mary in the garden and the disciples on the road to Emmaus encounter him but are unable recognize him at first. He is the same but different, real but changed.

He is the "firstfruits of those who have fallen asleep," the "firstborn from among the dead" and the "pioneer and perfecter" of our faith (1 Cor 15:20; Col 1:18; Heb 12:2). How he is now, so we shall be in the resurrection (1 Cor 15:21-26). Resurrection is a hope, not an everyday experience. No one has experienced the resurrection and come back to tell about it. It remains for us the grand mystery toward which our lives are even now being drawn.

Unlike the crucifixion of Jesus, of which we have hundreds of thousands of artistic depictions from ancient, medieval and modern times, renderings of the resurrection are rare. Down through the ages, few artists have attempted to represent the resurrection event. According to Roland Bainton, there are no extant pictorial representations of it from the first thousand years of Christian history.[2] Even today it is not a subject of regular artistic consideration. Artists have shied from the resurrection for many reasons: out of reverence, fear, lack of imagination or simply because they are confounded by the challenge of translating the resurrected Lord into mediums of paint, marble, charcoal or wood. Even in the New Testament, the appearance of the risen one

---

[2]Roland H. Bainton, *Behold the Christ* (New York: Harper & Row, 1974), p. 165.

creates commotion. Thomas drops to his knees and exclaims "My Lord and my God!"; Paul is forcibly unsaddled from his donkey; John of Patmos passes out.

The resurrection event is unexpected, uncontained, unparalleled, and, in the words of a great twentieth-century theologian, Hans Urs von Balthasar, "without analogy."[3] Without analogy? Balthasar cites five separate academic sources in support of his claim, but that does not patent it true. Stories about gods who die and rise again litter the annals of religious history and folklore. The resurrection of Jesus is not without precedent or analogy.

In fact, the first human civilization to leave written records, the Sumerians—the same civilization that Abram and Sarai and Lot would one day put behind them—venerated the goddess Inanna, "queen of heaven," who was reputed to have returned from death. Inanna, sometimes depicted as an eight-pointed star, or rosette, once detached herself from her celestial home and descended like mist to the earth and into the darkly graveled underworld of the dead. When her ethereal presence was discovered among the dead, she was forced to her knees, stripped, turned into a bloody corpse and hung from a stake. There the queen remained for three days and three nights, lifeless. Finally, two creatures sent by Enki, the god of wisdom, sprinkled food of life and water of life on Inanna's suspended corpse and restored her.[4] But the queen of heaven's ordeal left a vivid impression on the Sumerian people. The soul preparing for entrance into death's domain was advised to recite the prayer, "May Inanna be my vanguard."[5]

Other tales of divine death and resurrection abound in ancient cultures. The Eleusinian Mysteries had Persephone, the Egyptians Osiris, the Greeks Dionysus and the Norsemen Balder, all deities who suffered the grave and came back. So, is Christianity just another elaborate cult of the dying and rising god? Is Jesus just another reincarnation of Osiris,

---

[3]Hans Urs von Balthasar, *Mysterium Paschale*, trans. A. Nichols (San Francisco: Ignatius Press, 2000), p. 194.

[4]Samuel Kramer, *Sumerian Mythology*, rev. ed. (Philadelphia: University of Pennsylvania Press, 1972), pp. 86-87.

[5]Caitlin Barrett, "Was Dust Their Food and Clay Their Bread?" *Journal of Ancient Near Eastern Religions* 7, no. 1 (2007): 24.

Balder and Inanna? What is so different about *this* story and *this* Christ? These are difficult and serious questions that deserve much greater consideration than we can offer here. But we can quote C. S. Lewis, who most famously articulated the difference between the ancient myths of the dying and rising gods and the biblical testimonies to Jesus the Christ:

> The heart of Christianity is a myth which is also a fact. The old myth of the Dying God, without ceasing to be myth, comes down from the heaven of legend and imagination to the earth of history. It *happens*—at a particular date, in a particular place, followed by definable historical consequences. We pass from a Balder or an Osiris, dying nobody knows when or where, to a historical Person crucified (it is all in order) *under Pontius Pilate.*[6]

In the death and resurrection of Jesus, the fleeting Egyptian gold of former myths becomes the substantive milk and honey of life. Here the myth does not simply touch upon or explains some aspect of reality; the myth of god entering the human cosmos becomes reality. In so doing, it alters reality. And so, von Balthasar may in fact be right: there is no real analogy for the resurrection. Here our analogies fail; I spy more unlikeness than likeness. Christ made alive is in some ways *like* a story, *like* a myth, *like* a narrative, *like* a drama—but it is also much, much more. All comparisons and parallels are but shadows of the real thing. The comparison is between the stuff of dreams and the blinding light of day, between an imaginary mirage and the actual oasis. When the risen Lord stepped out of the mouth of the tomb, when he planted his newly-restored foot on the dewy ground for the first time and he exhaled his first breath, everything changed because the "myth" was living fact.

Peter Chrysologus (c. 380–450), Latin archbishop of Ravenna, intercedes on our behalf,

> Pray, brothers, that the angel would descend now and roll away all the hardness of our hearts and open up our closed senses and declare to our minds that Christ has risen, for just as the heart in which Christ lives

---

[6]C. S. Lewis, *God in the Dock* (Grand Rapids: Eerdmans, 1970, 2001), pp. 66-67.

and reigns is heaven, so also the heart in which Christ remains dead and buried is a grave. May it be believed that just as he died, so was he transformed. Christ the man suffered, died and was buried; as God, he lives, reigns, is and will be forever.[7]

The resurrection is not some fact to be tacked on to the end of Jesus' biography, like an episode of VH-1's *Where Are They Now?* Nor is resurrection the warm milk and cookies we get after a heart-wrenching tale of tragedy: "The resurrection of Christ is not another event *after* his passion and death . . . the resurrection is the manifestation of what happened in the death of Christ."[8] As we hear the angel declare that Christ has risen, we find that our hearts are transformed. The resurrection lets us know that God's will has gone into effect, that the death has made a difference, and that Jesus had accomplished what he came to accomplish. Hans Urs von Balthasar adds, "The whole New Testament is unanimous on this point: the Cross and burial of Christ reveal their significance only in the light of the event of Easter, without which there is no Christian faith."[9] Because of this, the resurrection of Jesus cannot be just one more fact about the way things are; it transforms us personally as it transforms the whole New Testament story. The restoration to life of the Son of God is the twist of the story that turns the plot around and sets it on a different trajectory.

ACT 5: CHURCH

The finality of the resurrection and ascension of Christ who "is seated at the right hand of the Father" and "will come again in glory to judge the living and the dead," as the Nicene Creed states (echoing 1 Pet 3:22 and elsewhere), is not quite as final as it sounds. Followers of the risen one still live in between the times. The Word has been spoken from eternity and has been seen in history, but the sound of it is still on its way and has not yet reached our ears. In the same way

---

[7]Peter Chrysologus *Sermon* 75.4, quoted in *Ancient Christian Devotional: Lectionary Cycle A*, ed. Thomas Oden and Cindy Crosby (Downers Grove, Ill.: InterVarsity Press, 2007), p. 103.

[8]Karl Rahner, quoted in Nicholas Lash, *Theology on the Way to Emmaus* (London: SCM Press, 1986), p. 180.

[9]Balthasar, *Mysterium Paschale*, p. 189.

that we first see lightning or fireworks and after a delay hear the boom, so the incarnation, death and resurrection have already occurred and yet the reverberations are still being heard and felt. We have seen the manger and the grave emptied, but still wait to hear the trumpet of resurrection. Deeds take time, and the biggest deeds take the most time.

The story of Christ is incomplete, or better, not-yet-complete. This is where we, the church, the followers of the Way, find ourselves in the story. More than one artist has departed this world leaving works unfinished. Charles Dickens died in 1870 while publishing monthly installments of a novel called *The Mystery of Edwin Drood*. Unfortunately, he left no clue as to how the last three hundred pages or so should go. A number of people writing by the "spirit pen of Charles Dickens" could not resist the urge to help him posthumously finish the work. Mozart likewise died leaving what is arguably one of his most haunting musical achievements, the *Requiem Mass in D Minor*, unfinished. Plagued by illness, delusions and an awareness of his approaching demise, Mozart left details with regards to the completion of the music for Süssmayr. After he succumbed to death in December of 1791 in Vienna, his confidant Süssmayr did complete the Requiem, but not without the help of two other pupils of Mozart named Freystädtler and Eybler. Orchestras wanting to perform the Requiem must decide whether to restrict themselves to what Mozart himself wrote or include Süssmayr's additions. They must also decide what to do with Eybler's contributions, which were cut from the arrangement by Süssmayr.

The end of Jesus' story is not like that of either Dickens or Mozart, as fascinating as those stories are. It is much more like that of Karl Barth, the famous Swiss Protestant theologian who died at the mature age of eighty-two. In his last year the question was already being raised by others in public and published formats, "Is Barth obsolete?" to which the wizened saint could only chuckle. He agreed to speak on a Swiss radio program a month before his death and said, "The last word which I have to say as a theologian and also as a politician is not a term like 'grace,' but a name, 'Jesus Christ.' He is grace, and he is the last, beyond the world and the church and even theology."[10]

On the evening of December 9, 1968, as Eberhard Busch retells the story, Barth was working on a lecture when the phone rang. After a conversation with his dearest old friend, Eduard Thurneysen, Barth hung up but did not return to his lecture. He saved it for another day and went to bed. His wife discovered the next morning as she tried to wake him with the sounds of Mozart playing in the background that he had died peacefully in the night. The draft of the lecture was left unfinished. The last line of the partially completed lecture trails off in an incomplete sentence: "'God is not a God of the dead but of the living.' In him they all live."[11] It is a wonderful line. The sentence may be incomplete but the thought is not. In him they all live.

The tale of Jesus does not have a terminus, an ending, a final sentence with a final period. Here we find the opposite of most storytelling patterns. Stories typically begin *in medias res*, in the middle of events. Significant action has already occurred when the story begins, which must be explained by way of flashbacks or character conversations. This device is a way of catching the attention of the audience, by plunging them directly into the thick of the plot. But the narrative of Jesus reverses the expected pattern. While Jesus' narrative has a definite beginning, "in the beginning was the Word," it has no definite ending. It ends *in medias res*.

Neither Matthew nor John concludes with an ascension or final disappearance of Jesus. While Jesus' final ascension to the right hand of the Father is alluded to in both Matthew and John (Mt 26:64 and Jn 6:62; 14:2; 20:17), the narrative nonetheless stops after the risen Lord appears to the disciples (Jn 20:30–21:25) and commands them to spread out and announce the news of his resurrection (Mt 28:16-20). Luke offers a more rounded conclusion with Jesus being "taken up into heaven" and the disciples returning to Jerusalem "praising God" (Lk 24:51-53). Mark, by far the most striking and sudden, finishes the last scene of action with Mary Magdalene, Mary the mother of James and

---

[10]Eberhard Busch, *Karl Barth: His Life from Letters and Autobiographical Texts*, trans. John Bowden (Philadelphia: Fortress, 1976), p. 496.

[11]Ibid., p. 498.

Salome scattering from the empty tomb. Having met not Jesus but a "young man dressed in a white robe" and been told that Jesus is not dead but alive, the women stumble away frightened and amazed. In his excited if wobbly Greek, Mark writes, "Trembling and bewildered, the women went out and fled from the tomb. They said nothing to anyone, because they were afraid" (Mk 16:8).[12] With the exception of Luke, who narrates the ascension both in his Gospel and in his second volume, the Acts of the Apostles, the Gospels end unresolved almost, with one foot in the air—quite literally, open ended.

This is not to say that Matthew, Mark and John did not affirm the ascension of Jesus to the right hand of the Father. Like Luke, they certainly do affirm it; in fact, the ascension is an integral part of their understanding of the incarnation. McGill University professor Douglas Farrow has taken great pains to demonstrate the biblical and theological centrality of the ascension in his 1999 book *Ascension and Ecclesia: On the Significance of the Doctrine of the Ascension for Ecclesiology and Christian Cosmology*.[13] If the ascension *does* indeed play a central role in the cosmology and theology of the Gospel writers, all the more reason to think it significant that they conclude their accounts *without* a nice and tidy ending, that is, without a detailed account of the ascension. They do not wrap everything up with Jesus drifting through an opening in the clouds, disappearing from sight. That is

---

[12]In point of fact, Mk 16:19 does record that "he was taken up into heaven and he sat at the right hand of God." There is considerable discussion among scholars about the original ending of Mark. The modern exegete Joel Marcus asserts that although verses 9-20 appear in our modern translations, "they were almost certainly not penned by Mark, nor were they the original ending of the Gospel":

> Verses 9-20, moreover, do not exist in our earliest and best Greek manuscripts, Sinaiticus and Vaticanus, both of which terminate at 16:8, as do the Sinaitic Syriac, about a hundred Armenian manuscripts, the two oldest Georgian manuscripts (from 897 and 913 C.E.), and all but one manuscript of the Sahidic Coptic. When verses 9-20 do appear, moreover, they are often separated from 16:8 by scribal signs (asterisks or obeli) or by notations that state or suggest that what follows is not found in some witnesses. (pp. 1088-89)

For these and other points to consider, see Joel Marcus, *Mark 8–16*, Anchor Yale Bible 27A (New Haven, Conn.: Yale University Press, 2009), pp. 1088-96. Craig Evans agrees, although he gives less information on the subject (*Mark 8:27–16:20*, Word Biblical Commentary 34B [Nashville: Thomas Nelson, 2001], pp. 540-52).

[13]Douglas Farrow, *Ascension and Ecclesia* (Grand Rapids: Eerdmans, 1999). Appreciation goes to an anonymous reviewer who directed me to this source.

the way Acts *begins*, but not how Matthew, Mark and John *end*.

I think it's not coincidental that we are left with the question: What comes next?

The after-story of Jesus is the continuation or the fulfillment or the realization of the Jesus' life and ministry, death and resurrection, descent and ascent. What comes next is the church, the body of Christ empowered by the Spirit to carry out the work of Jesus. Life in the Spirit means living out the terms of the last will and testament of the one who died but is now glorified. Irenaeus declares at the conclusion of the little handbook he wrote to introduce the Christian message:

> This, beloved, is the preaching of the truth, and this is the character of our salvation, and this is the way of life, which the prophets announced and Christ confirmed and the apostles handed over and the Church, in the whole world, hands down to her children.[14]

The will of God is that the church becomes the true body (*corpus verum*) of Christ for the world. Christ is broken for us so that we might be broken for the world.[15] Christ is given to us so that we might give Christ to the world. The story is not something meant to be kept for oneself, told in secret or hidden from view. It is meant to be shared, given away, handed over. Christians are most appropriately called "witnesses," for we testify to extraordinary events. Indeed, we are commanded to tell and retell the story, as often as needed, until he comes.

ACT 6: CONSUMMATION

Death may be the unavoidable last word for us, but God speaks one more word after it. In Christ life is made new. The end of our story is not the end. The End of the Christian narrative is a whole new story: meeting our Lord in the resurrection to life. Midway through his second missionary journey, a weather-worn Paul entered Athens and paid a visit to the ethereal philosophers of the Areopagus. They must have presented quite a spectacle; some wore specially dyed philosopher's

---

[14]Irenaeus, *On Apostolic Preaching*, 98, trans. by John Behr (Crestwood, N.Y.: St. Vladimir's Seminary Press, 1997), p. 100.
[15]Cavanaugh, *Torture and Eucharist*, pp. 231-33.

cloaks, some went barefoot in imitation of Socrates, some wore plain, coarse tunics like Diogenes, but all "spent their time doing nothing but talking about and listening to the latest ideas" (Acts 17:21). Then there was Paul, described in an early record as a squat man with a balding head, a protrusive nose and a classic unibrow.[16] His unfortunate appearance would not have bothered the philosophers; it might have even endeared him to them—after all, Socrates was depicted as pug-nosed and potbellied.

At any rate, the odd, Jewish-born wayfarer from Tarsus preached passionately to the gathered men as they reclined in the shade of the milky marble colonnades, winning them over with quotations from Posidonius and Aratus. All went well until his talk was interrupted by the sounds of snickering and throat-clearing. Paul stopped midsentence, his train of thought broken by the noise and the murmuring, and was informed that his mention of the resurrection had set off his listeners. They were saying, "Yes, of course the soul is immortal . . . but not the body. Everyone knows that. You can't seriously believe that the same physical body will be reproduced one day after death for the eternal soul to inhabit? Absurd!" The titter and chatter of the intellectuals swelled to such a din that Paul had to be asked to return on a different day to finish his talk. As far as we know, he never did. But a presentation of the Christian doctrine of resurrection *was* eventually delivered to the Athenians—over a hundred years later.

Athenagoras (d. 180) picked up the gauntlet sometime in the second half of the second century. Originally from Athens, Athenagoras crossed the Mediterranean to become head of the Catechetical School of Alexandria, where he wore "the philosopher's garb" and trained Christian intellectuals to read Scripture and defend the faith. Thinking perhaps of how the lighthouse at Alexandria's port (one of the seven wonders of the ancient world) throws its light across the sea, Athenagoras decided to throw a treatise on the resurrection across the sea to the Athenians and finish Paul's speech. His name, Athenagoras, is it-

---

[16]The author of *The Acts of Thecla* tries to soften this unflattering portrait by adding that at least his face was "full of grace." *The Acts of Thecla* 3, in *Lost Scriptures*, ed. Bart Ehrman (New York: Oxford University Press, 2003), p. 114.

self a combination of *Athens* and *agora,* Greek for the "marketplace" where Athenians went to buy daily fish and food as well as exchange news, gossip, politics and ideas—and this, the *agora,* is just the right setting for his short masterpiece of rhetoric and reason. Athenagoras wanted to address the makers and marketers of ideas in Athens. Like Paul before him, he directed the attention of the Athenians to that "Unknown God" who is the true author and finisher of the cosmos:

> It is the act of one and the same power to give shape to what is customarily regarded by these philosophers as shapeless matter, to arrange into many and varied patterns what was shapeless and disorderly, to unite into one the parts of the elements, to divide into many the seed that is one and simple, to make articulate what is not so, and to give life to that which has it not; and, on the other hand, to unite what has been dissolved, to raise up what has been laid low, to restore the dead to life and to change the corruptible into incorruption.[17]

If the power of God is sufficient to press matter into life, is it not also sufficient to reconstitute that life? As Athenagoras's contemporary Tatian wrote, "We were not created to die."[18] We were created to live, and to enjoy our Creator for all eternity. "Praise him for his acts of power" (Ps 150:2).

St. Antony, a devout monk, lived in the deserts and mountains of Egypt and was revered by everyone. Before he died in 356, he exhorted his disciples not to preserve his body unburied, as was the custom of some who liked to visit and admire the bodies of saints and martyrs. Antony wanted to be buried in earth common to all. He asked that no one apart from those who buried him know his place of rest.[19] Christians are not to obsess over dead bodies, but to look for the resurrection. Ours is a faith in life, not a memorial to death. We are not "to grieve as others do who have no hope" (1 Thess 4:13 NRSV). We are not to cling to this present body, but to that other body that can save—Christ's body.

---

[17]Athenagoras *The Resurrection of the Dead* 3, Ancient Christian Writers, vol. 23 (New York: Newman Press, 1955), p. 83.

[18]Tatian *Address of Tatian to the Greeks* 11, ANF, vol. 2, p. 69.

[19]Athanasius *Life of Antony* 90-91, in *Early Christian Lives,* ed. Carolinne White (London: Penguin, 1998), pp. 66-67.

In John's Gospel, Jesus tells Martha, bleary-eyed with grief over her dead brother Lazarus, "I am the resurrection and the life. He who believes in me will live, *even though he dies*" (Jn 11:25, emphasis mine). Death is not the end, but the beginning. In the end is life.[20] This is a strange saying indeed, because dying is not living and living is not dying. Resurrection in Christ is not an end but an ongoing—a flourishing, recreation, renewal and rebirth that fulfills and surpasses all other births, creations and existences.

"Lazarus, come out!"

---

[20]This is a prominent theme in Irenaeus. "He, the same against whom we had sinned in the beginning, grants forgiveness of sins in the end . . . as our species went down to death through a vanquished man, so we may ascend to life again through a victorious one; and as through a man death received the palm [of victory] against us, so again by a man we may receive the palm against death" (*Against Heresies* 5.20-21, ANF, vol. 1, pp. 545, 549).

CHRISTIANITY AS LANGUAGE

6

CHRISTIANITY AS LANGUAGE

LANGUAGE TRAINING

Speak to me so that I may hear.

See the ears of my heart are before you, Lord.

Open them and "say to my soul, I am your salvation."

After that utterance I will run and lay hold on you.

AUGUSTINE

To BEGIN WITH, WE HEARD the Christian faith as a story. This was the right way to start. We need to understand the basic plotline, characters and trajectory of the Christian story before we can go anywhere else. Oddly enough, though, as we worked our way through the narrative of creation, catastrophe, covenant, Christ, church and consummation, we were not only learning a plot, we were learning how to speak a divine language: God's Word. The process of getting our story straight was the beginning of our language training. The Christian language molds itself around a narrative—the Jesus narrative. In this chapter, we will consider what this means and how Christianity resembles a language.

Language makes for a fascinating comparison with Christianity. I want to highlight five ways in which the Christian faith can be compared to a language. After expanding on each of these, I plan to number four ways in which it does not compare to a language.

✛ First, language is open to all people. In principle, anyone can learn a new language; it cannot be "owned" by any one person or group. It is free to all who have ears to hear and tongues to speak. Likewise is Christianity open to all people; anyone can "join." The message is not owned by any one person or group (despite the arrogant claims of a few); it is free to all who have ears to hear and tongues to speak.

The apostle Peter was one of the first to learn this lesson. The rugged but big-hearted fisherman knew the rules of his Jewish faith like he knew the rules of the water: self-respecting, clean Jews were not supposed to mix with dirty Gentiles. But after receiving a dramatic rooftop vision challenging his ideas about hygiene and then a personal invitation to visit the house of a non-Jew, he began to rethink those rules. He agreed to go with the men sent from Cornelius the Gentile. When he arrived at Cornelius' house, he made his reservations known, "You are well aware that it is against our law for a Jew to associate with a Gentile or visit him." One can imagine him opening his palms and admitting somewhat begrudgingly, "But God has shown me that I should not call any man impure or unclean" (Acts 10:28). Cornelius was not deterred by this Jewish fisherman's less-than-enthusiastic attitude. He reported the sequence of events that led him to call for Peter. To his credit, Peter listened intently—and his mind was changed. "I now realize how true it is that God does not show favoritism but accepts men from every nation who fear him and do what is right" (Acts 10:34-35). The Holy Spirit descended upon Cornelius and his household just as he did upon Peter and his fellow Jewish believers, causing Peter to exclaim, "Can anyone keep these people from being baptized with water? They have received the Holy Spirit just as we have" (Acts 10:47).

✛ So Christianity, like language, is no respecter of persons. Christianity is similar to a language in another sense, too. Language may be equally accessible to all, but its skills are not naturally or easily acquired. Learning a language takes time and effort, discipline and training. Children and adults alike must work at it. It involves repetition, examination and practice. In the same way, the faithful practice of Christian belief requires patience, discipline, practice and outside help. Christianity comes with its own vocabulary, its own sounds and its own way of communicating verbally and nonverbally. All these things must be learned and absorbed.[1] Speaking the Christian tongue requires work. With time and devotion and the Spirit's nurturing help, the learner becomes competent in the language, "so that everyone who belongs to God may be proficient" (2 Tim 3:17). Some are even able to master the faith with fluency—we call such people "saints." Others will always struggle with the language of faith and speak it haltingly. Gregory of Nyssa articulates the challenge in his treatise "On Perfection":

> Therefore, since, thanks to our good Master, we are sharers of the greatest and the most divine and the first of names, those honored by the name of Christ being called Christians, it is necessary that there be seen in us also all the connotations of this name, so that the title be not a misnomer in our case, but that our life be a testimony of it.[2]

Gregory goes on to describe what kind of effort we must put forth so that the moniker "Christian" is not a misnomer. Gregory also realized that more than sheer willpower and effort, the Christian life also requires education,[3] which brings us to a third comparison with language.

✦ A person cannot learn French by simply *wanting* to learn French, she must be *taught*. Language training requires teachers and experts—grammarians, teachers, professors, editors—individuals who have a mastery of the language and know the technical rules of the language and are able to communicate and instruct others in those rules. Christianity likewise requires teachers and experts—parents, Sunday school leaders, youth ministers, pastors, deacons and elders, university and seminary professors. Christianity must be taught. "How, then, can they

---

[1]See Kathleen Norris, *Amazing Grace: A Vocabulary of Faith* (New York: Riverhead, 1999).
[2]Gregory of Nyssa *On Perfection*, Fathers of the Church, vol. 58 (Washington, D.C.: Catholic University of America Press, 1967), p. 98.
[3]Ibid., pp. 110-11.

call on the one they have not believed in? And how can they believe in the one of whom they have not heard? And how can they hear without someone preaching to them?" (Rom 10:14). The feet of those bringing good news truly are a beautiful sight.

Sometimes, the teaching of the Christian faith literally takes the form of teaching a new language, or perhaps even inventing one. In A.D. 862, two brothers from Thessalonica were selected by the patriarch of Constantinople to spread the gospel of Jesus to the untamed Slavic tribes of the north. There was only one problem for the talented and well-educated Cyril (c. 826–869) and his monkish brother Methodius (c. 815–885).[4] The Slavs had no written language—not even a discernible alphabet. Of course, they had a spoken language, but there is considerable difference between a spoken and a written language (just ask the Chinese!). Apparently, the Slavic people of Moravia (now the Czech Republic) did not feel the need to put things in writing. The two brothers from Thessalonica felt differently.

Using his knowledge of Greek and Hebrew, Cyril constructed a forty-letter alphabet, called Glagolitic, for the purpose of translating the Gospels and other edifying and liturgical texts into the Slavic tongue. The new written language would be known as Old Church Slavonic, and it would have a long-lasting influence on the church and cultural development of the Slavic and Russian peoples. Even today, some Orthodox churches still read and chant from Cyril's translations. For their efforts, Cyril and his brother would not only be remembered as saints, but honored with the status of co-equals with the apostles.[5] The work of translating, interpreting and teaching the faith is essential and indispensable.

---

[4]The Cyril here is not the same Cyril of Jerusalem mentioned elsewhere in this text. Cyril's given name was Constantine (he is sometimes known as Constantine the Philosopher). Methodius's may have been Michael. The brothers assumed names other than their given ones to show their commitment to God and their vows (Colin Wells, *Sailing from Byzantium* [New York: Delacorte Press, 2006], pp. 189-95).

[5]In modern times, Sequoyah, the Cherokee Indian from Tennessee, can be credited with an equally stupendous achievement. Despite being illiterate in the English language, he generated a syllabary of over eighty characters, some borrowed from the Roman alphabet and some invented, in order to represent the different sounds of the Cherokee language. With his syllabary, he hammered out a workable language system for the Cherokees.

✚ Fourth, speaking a language is a communal activity. It works in group settings. Language bridges the gap between people, creates understanding, allows for the exchange of ideas and so on. Language directs and connects one person to another. Language is meant to be shared. Christian commitment is meant to be shared, too. It is to be lived in relation to God and then to God's people, the church, and after that to other people beyond the doors of the church. Think of Jesus' two great commandments: love God and love neighbor (Mt 22:37; Mk 12:30; Lk 10:27). Both commandments are relational, neither can be performed in solitude. A private Christianity is just as much an anomaly as a private language.[6]

The foreign language that was learned in high school but never spoken after graduation soon fades into oblivion. Why? Because it needs to be practiced and exercised. So also a Christian faith that is never expressed or communicated or matured soon disintegrates and disappears. Sadly, the failure of a new decision for Christ is usually the failure of community. If a new believer does not tie into a worshipping community or a discipleship group, he or she will soon drop the whole idea and never be seen again.

✚ Fifth, comparing Christianity to a language helps us to overcome the imaginary division between sacred and secular, holy and profane, spiritual and ordinary. Language does not recognize such boundaries. One speaks the same English language whether buying groceries or grieving over a lost love or reporting to the boss. Faith likewise should not recognize human boundaries. The same faith should attend all situations and fields of life. Certainly, language expresses itself differently depending on the circumstances—there is a difference between grocery shopping and grieving. The faith also comports itself differently at different times—there is a difference between conducting a Bible study and conducting the sale of a house. And yet, faith is present and can be articulated in both settings.

---

[6]Ludwig Wittgenstein, *Philosophical Investigations,* 3rd ed. (New York: Macmillan, 1968), §§243-75.

The point is that just as our mother tongue is intimately connected with our personal identity, so our vow to Jesus Christ should be intimately connected with who we are. It identifies us through and through—all the way down. We cannot set the cross aside in order to perform an activity or fulfill a role any more than we can set aside our native tongue whenever we like. It is possible to deny Christ before others, just as it is possible for me to deny to someone that I am an English speaker. But both denials are lies. Peter denied Christ three times, and all three denials were lies for which he was immediately sorry (Mk 14:30-72).

We have outlined in detail five similarities between language and Christianity. We now need to balance our comparison by identifying three points of dissimilarity.

■ The comparison between language and Christianity tends to be reductionistic. If we overemphasize the analogy, we might give the impression that Christian theology is nothing more than a language game, a play on words, a chance to toy with vocabulary. The apostle Paul was wary of words and their ability to sedate, confuse, distract and deceive. He wrote to the church at Corinth—that carnival of a city that regularly entertained the Olympic games, "I did not come with eloquence or superior wisdom. . . . My message and my preaching were not with wise and persuasive words, but with a demonstration of the Spirit's power" (1 Cor 2:1, 4). In other words, *I did not play games with you or trick you with rhetoric.* The kingdom of God is not built on words, but actions. Christianity is not so many words, but power and reality.

■ Language is a human construction. Humans invent words and grammar; by natural and normal powers humans learn to speak, read and write. Christian belief, on the other hand, is a gift from God's Spirit. The Christian faith is not the product of human minds, but the gift of the almighty's revelation and grace. "For the grace of God that brings salvation has appeared to all men" (Tit 2:11) and "it is by grace you have been saved, through faith—and this not from yourselves, it is the gift of God" (Eph 2:8). My fear of the language analogy is that it offers very few points of entry for divine action and revelation.

■ On a similar note, languages are malleable and mutable, the Christian gospel is not. Languages are always changing, mutating and evolving. They discard old verbs, nouns and adjectives and adopt new ones naturally and without trouble. But Christian revelation is characterized by its eternal, lasting quality. It cannot be edited, jettisoned, adapted, enhanced or added to without seriously jeopardizing its integrity. Certainly, our task is to always find new ways to express and embody the faith we profess—but that's just it—you and I *profess* the faith, we don't *possess* it. It belongs to God the Father, his Son and the Spirit. We have no right to tinker with the essentials, picking and choosing as we like.

7

CHRISTIANITY AS LANGUAGE

LEARNING A NEW TONGUE

WHEN IT COMES TO TALKING ABOUT GOD, it goes without saying that we must be extra careful about the words we choose and the manner in which we use them.[1] Is God "the man upstairs," "the hand of fate," "the supreme and immovable judge" or "the divine mechanic"? Words make all the difference.

Sometimes we misspeak about God in self-serving ways. We like to put God on our team and speak of God in words we understand, approve of and can control. Or, we may prefer to distance God from us with our words and portray divinity as something as far off as the moon. However, there is a deeper and more perplexing problem than this. Even if we act with a pure heart and a right mind, the truth is that whenever we name God we are still trying to give expression to something, or more properly, someone, who is beyond expression and who overwhelms all depictions. There just are not enough words. Even if we could gather up all the right kind of words, it would still be a job for Sisyphus.

Describing God with words—any kind of words—is like trying to dry up the ocean with a kitchen sponge. It doesn't matter how big your sponge is or how long you work at it. Pseudo-Dionysius, writing in the late fifth century about the divine names (his life dates are unknown), reminds us that

---

[1]A theologian, as Gerald O'Collins has said, is someone who "watches his language in the presence of God." Quoted in Nicholas Lash, *Easter in Ordinary* (Notre Dame, Ind.: University of Notre Dame Press, 1988), p. 12.

just as the senses can neither grasp nor perceive the things of the mind, just as representation and shape cannot take in the simple and the shape-less, just as corporal form cannot lay hold of the intangible and incorpo-real, by the same standard of truth beings are surpassed by the infinity beyond being, intelligences by that oneness which is beyond intelli-gence. Indeed the inscrutable One is out of the reach of every rational process. Nor can any words come up to the inexpressible Good, this One, this Source of all unity, this supra-existent Being. Mind beyond mind, word beyond speech.[2]

No one has (or should have) an easy time talking about God; this is *God* we are talking about, not a vacuum cleaner.[3] We modern Western-ers find it especially difficult to relate to God or even talk about God because we have a particularly hard time dealing with mystery, abstrac-tion and spirit. We don't care for airy thought projects; we like ideas with practical applications and immediate results. The late French phi-losopher of inestimable repute and inordinate controversy, Jacques Der-rida (1930–2004), spent his career investigating the consequences of this fact.

Best known as the proponent of "deconstruction," Derrida wrote prolifically and lectured widely, both in France and in the States. Of the many observations he made about life and learning, his greatest is probably that the basic pattern of thinking in modern, Western societ-ies is binary. We think in twos. Europeans and Americans fundamen-tally conceive of everything in pairs, for example: simple-complex, beautiful-ugly, male-female, white-black, inside-outside, true-false, mind-body, good-bad, God-Satan, fact-fiction, forward-backward, presence-absence.

The list of binary sets could be extended in any direction. Not only do we tend to divide everything up into twos, Derrida contends that we

---

[2]Pseudo-Dionysius *The Divine Names* 1.1, in *Pseudo-Dionysius: The Complete Works,* trans. Colm Luibheid (New York: Paulist Press, 1987), pp. 49-50.

[3]Jean-Luc Marion places an *X* over the name of G×d in his text so as to remind his readers that "we are not at all speaking of 'God' in general. . . . We are speaking of the G×d who is crossed by a cross because he reveals himself by his placement on a cross, the G×d revealed by, in, and as the Christ" (*God Without Being,* trans. Thomas Carlson [Chicago: University of Chicago Press, 1991], p. 71).

value and emphasize one to the detriment of the other. We value things that are beautiful, white, true, good and factual, and disapprove of things that are ugly, black, false, bad and fictional.[4] The first set of things can be characterized as virtuous, profitable, essential and accessible, whereas the second set represents what is lacking, morally deficient, nonessential or nonexistent. No one wants to spend time with things that are complex, ugly, bodily, backward or absent.

Much of Derrida's work attempts to expose and disturb this bias by invading it with "the face of the Other," that Other being non-Westerners, minority groups, women, the underprivileged, the forgotten.[5] Derrida personally experienced otherness and alienation, first at the age of twelve when, in 1942, he was expelled from his school by French administrators enforcing anti-Semitic quotas, and later from the Sephardic Jewish community when he skipped school for a year rather than attend the Jewish lycée (he kept up appearances during this time by pretending to learn Hebrew). His experiences in life as an outsider and dissident opened his eyes to larger ideas and patterns of thought that alienate or are alienated.

At the heart of his ambitions is a commitment to undermine the exclusionary logic of binaries. Derrida wants to explode our preference for thinking in twos, our insatiable need to divide everything out into easy, either-or options. He goes to great lengths to show us how gifts, for instance, can disrupt the economy of equal exchange. What is more uncomfortable than being given a gift for no particular reason and not being able to reciprocate? Indecision disrupts the yes or no pattern of decision making. What is more frustrating than a friend who refuses to decide where to eat, or what kind of food to eat, but, when asked, simply shrugs his shoulders and says, "Whatever"? Forgiveness disrupts the equalizing logic of retribution and payback. What is more difficult than to say, "I forgive you," and not extract retribution for a wrong? Mourning disrupts the raw facts of life and death. What is more dis-

---

[4]He calls this disposition a "metaphysics of presence" (Jacques Derrida, *Of Grammatology*, trans. Gayatri Chakravorty Spivak [Baltimore, Md.: Johns Hopkins University Press, 1974], p. 49).
[5]Jacques Derrida, *The Ear of the Other: Otobiography, Transference, Translation*, trans. Peggy Kamuf, ed. Christie McDonald (New York: Schocken Books, 1985).

comforting than someone who refuses to stop grieving for a lost loved one?[6] The truth is that we like things to be predictable, fair and stable. The traces, cracks and fissures that emerge in the form of gifts, undecidability, forgiveness and mourning threaten the satisfying balance of equal exchange.

THE EFFECTS OF
BINARY THINKING ON THEOLOGY

Much God-talk has been squeezed through the same kind of binary presses that Derrida notices in Western philosophy. Discourse on God usually happens in one of two ways or in a combination thereof. Language about God is either affirmative or negative—or to use much older categories: *cataphatic* or *apophatic*. Affirmative, cataphatic statements might be "God is love" and "God is one" and "God is light." Examples of negative, apophatic statements are "God is not hate" and "God is not divided" and "There is no darkness in God." In a sense, these two sets of statements represent two ways of saying the same thing. "God is love" is an affirmation; "God is not hate" is a negation. But in truth, they do not say exactly the same thing. They are different, even if complementary.

The terms *cataphatic* and *apophatic* come from Greek roots and were introduced best by Pseudo-Dionysius, or Denys the Areopagite, as he is variously known. This wonderfully mystical thinker styled himself in the persona of Dionysius, a member of the judicial council at Athens who converted to Christianity under the preaching of Paul. Adopting the name Dionysius allowed him to write both as a committed Pauline believer and as a Neo-Platonic Athenian. For the subtle and profound Dionysius, *cataphatic* refers to what can be known definitively by humans and asserted positively about God; *apophatic* refers to

---

[6]These cases are made over the course of a number of important texts, for instance, *On Cosmopolitanism and Forgiveness* (London: Routledge, 2001); *Circumfessions: Fifty Nine Periphrases*, in G. Bennington, *Jacques Derrida* (Chicago: University of Chicago Press, 1993); *Given Time: i. Counterfeit Money*, trans. Peggy Kamuf (Chicago: University of Chicago Press, 1992); *Politics of Friendship*, trans. George Collins (New York: Verso, 1997); *The Work of Mourning*, ed. Pascale-Anne Brault and Michael Nass (Chicago: University of Chicago Press, 2001); "Psyche: Inventions of the Other" in *Reading De Man Reading*, ed. Lindsey Waters and Wlad Godzich (Minneapolis: University of Minnesota Press, 1989).

what cannot be known or said about God, or what can be known through negation.

Readers in more modern times might prefer instead the adjectives *affirmative* and *negative*. By the way, these terms do not imply moral judgment, such that affirmative means good and negative bad. Rather, *affirmative* indicates a truth that can be identified and confirmed ("God knows everything; he is omniscient"), and *negative* denotes a denial or counteractive statement ("God is not mortal, that is, he cannot be killed"). In other words, there are some things we can "affirm" about God's character and other things we need to "negate."

Theologians over the ages have argued about the value of these two kinds of language. The mystical Dionysius contended that the most fitting and perfect way to discuss God's nature was apophatically, by way of negation, because God's nature is, in the final analysis, mystery-laden and unknowable to human minds. "God in his total transcendence is unlike anything else" and as such "remains inaccessible and beyond our grasp."[7] Although in God "there is understanding, reason, knowledge, touch, perception, imagination, name, and many other things," Dionysius makes clear that "he is not understood" in these things.[8] About God himself, "nothing can be said, he cannot be named. He is not one of the things that are."[9] This is not a pronouncement of atheism, but Dionysius's declaration of God's greatness—God creates everything that exists, but is not one of those things. God does not exist like anything else in creation. These apophatic declarations contain deep truths about God.

"I cannot begin this paragraph." These words are both true and false; they claim something that they themselves negate. "I cannot begin this paragraph" is itself a beginning. Our language about God is like that. Some of the most important things we say about God turn out to be denials. But denials can actually be a way of starting the conversation and laying the groundwork. When we deny that God is a supersized, pasty, white guy with bony fingers and a curly beard, we are doing more

---

[7]Pseudo-Dionysius *The Divine Names* 12.4; 13.3, pp. 127-29.
[8]Ibid., 7.3, pp. 108-9.
[9]Ibid., p. 109.

than pushing away one idea. Our denial of divine corporeality is also a way of affirming something about God—it affirms a different kind of divine presence than corporeal. We are not saying God is not *real*, we are saying that God's presence in the universe and in us is the presence of *spirit*—as real as any body, but different from any and every body.

The University of Paris regent master of theology, John Duns Scotus (1265/6–1308), argued in contrast to thinkers like Dionysius that *affirmative* statements, not denials, best get at the essence of God's being. One of the most important things we can and must say about God is that "God exists," which Duns Scotus understood to be a straightforward, cataphatic, or to use his language, "univocal," statement.[10] By "univocal" Duns Scotus means to say that the word "exists" means the same thing when applied to God as when applied to other beings. In an early work called *De Metaphysica*, he argues "that God cannot be known naturally unless being is univocal to the created and the uncreated."[11] The modern-day commentator Thomas Williams says that according to Duns Scotus, "there are concepts under whose extension both God and creatures fall, so that the corresponding predicate expressions are used with exactly the same sense in predications about God as in predications about creatures."[12] The value in affirming that at least some of the words we use to describe normal things can also be used to describe God in a genuine and true manner is that it saves us from a radical skepticism or agnosticism. If we are not permitted any confidence in our language, then how can we have confidence in our knowledge of God?

Duns Scotus ("Scotus" indicates that he was originally from Scotland—Maxton, Roxburgh, to be exact) felt that we must always start with the univocal. We must first have something to affirm before we can have something to deny. Affirmation is prior to negation; affirming that God exists comes *before* denying that God is a material being

---

[10]See Étienne Gilson, *History of Christian Philosophy in the Middle Ages* (New York: Random House, 1955), p. 456.

[11]John Duns Scotus, *De Metaphysica*, in *Philosophical Writings*, trans. Allan Wolter (Indianapolis: Hackett, 1987), p. 5.

[12]Thomas Williams, "The Doctrine of Univocity Is True and Salutary," *Modern Theology* 21, no. 4 (2005): 578.

capable of being known through empirical observation. Saying that
something *is* or *has being* has to be the most basic starting point: "It
extends to all that is not nothing."[13] Once we have established a certain
univocal common ground by saying what God *is*, then we can proceed
to "equivocation," that is, denials and negations—saying what God is
not (Duns Scotus preferred "equivocation" to "apophatic" just as he preferred "univocal" to "cataphatic").

There are benefits that come with affirmative or univocal and negative or equivocal uses of language. Both methods are noble ways of
getting at the truth about God. One provides theological precision and
confessional clarity and the other mystical receptivity and windows of
exploration. And yet, each comes with certain frustrations. Thomas
Aquinas (1225–1274) expressed his own irritation in the following passage: "This is not what people want to say when they talk about God.
When a man speaks of the 'living God' he does not simply want to say
that God is the cause of our life, or that he differs from a lifeless body."[14]
To speak of God as "living" is not simply to affirm certain essential
qualities or negate others. We are not simply saying God is the cause of
life or that he is different from a corpse. We are expressing faith, hope
and love. The temptation is to settle for easy definitions and divisions.
But on second look, they turn out not to be very useful.

When I was in high school a few of us from the youth group worked
our way through a discipleship manual, the title of which I have since
forgotten. One of the lessons discussed the attributes of God's nature
using words I had never seen before in my life: omniscient, omnipotent, omnipresent, immutable, immaterial and eternal. It's funny—one
would think those big words would have been a complete turnoff for a
teenager, but I was elated by them. I was *finally* being told *who* and
what God was in precise, scientific terms. To my young and unformed
mind, the biblical metaphors that describe God as a loud trumpet, the
Alpha and Omega, a strong tower, and so forth, were *at last* explained.

---

[13]John Duns Scotus *Opus Oxoniense* 1, 3, 2, quoted in Gordon Leff, *Medieval Thought* (Chicago:
Quadrangle Books, 1958), p. 265.
[14]Thomas Aquinas *Summa Theologiae* 1a.13.2, quoted in William Placher, *Domestication of
Transcendence* (Louisville, Ky.: Westminster John Knox, 1996), p. 28.

What they *really* meant was that God is omnipotent, eternal, omniscient, etc. As an adult, I now realize I had everything completely backwards. Back then, I was drawn to those abstract attributes because they struck me as "clear and distinct ideas" (as Descartes would say); they offered seemingly straightforward and scientific ways to distill and define divinity. As a young Christian, I thought I had found the essential meaning and could dispose of all those confusing and excessive biblical images.

The classical attributes, both univocal or cataphatic and equivocal or apophatic, have enormous appeal to analytical, data-oriented minds. "Just the facts, ma'am." We like the essential characteristics of God's nature put on an easy, one page, bullet-point handout. We want a deity without frills. I imagine Derrida shaking his head and saying (in a thick French accent), "This is exactly what I meant about binary thinking!" God is either *this* or *that*. It is all quite simple and so very pretentious.

The revelation of God shatters all human preconceptions and vain attempts to explain the divine nature in clear and distinct ideas. Blaise Pascal (1632–1662), the famous mathematician and author of *Pensées*, sewed into the lining of his jacket a scrap of parchment on which he recorded his experience of conversion as an adult. When the jacket was removed and opened up upon his death, these words were found:

> In the year of grace, 1654,
> On Monday, 23rd of November . . .
> From about half past ten in the evening until about half past
>   twelve,
> FIRE!
> God of Abraham, God of Isaac, God of Jacob, (Ex 3:6; Mt 22:32)
> not of the philosophers and scholars.
> Certitude. Certitude. Feeling. Joy. Peace.
> God of Jesus Christ.[15]

The experience of God is the experience of fire, not of sterile scientific proof. Fire not only ignites, heats and illuminates, it also consumes. The experience and worship of the living God burns up all that

---

[15]Marvin O'Connell, *Blaise Pascal: Reasons of the Heart* (Grand Rapids: Eerdmans, 1997).

one is, heart, mind, soul and body. The God of Abraham, Isaac and Jacob cannot be chalked out in positive and negative attributes with omni–s and –ilities.

TALKING ANALOGIES

Thomas Aquinas is surely one of the most important thinkers of the Christian faith, standing shoulder to shoulder with St. Paul and St. Augustine. He was canonized (made a saint) in 1323, fifty years after his death, and then much later given the honorary title of Angelic Doctor of Catholic Doctrine in 1879 by the Roman Catholic Church. He is not only revered by Roman Catholics, he is admired and emulated by Protestants and Orthodox Christians, among others. But he was almost prevented from ever becoming a theologian by his upstanding and well-to-do family, who held him against his will for two years to keep him from joining the Dominican order. They wished to steer him toward a more lucrative and respectable career, but Thomas would have none of it. When they finally gave up and released him, he immediately joined the Dominicans and was put on the road to the University of Paris, where Duns Scotus would likewise arrive in just a few years. After obtaining the necessary degrees, he began to give lectures and hold disputations at the university. Students flocked to him. For anyone with intellectual interests or ambitions, Paris was *the* place to be. The university was less than a hundred years old when Thomas began teaching. But already, the city's famous Left Bank and Latin Quarter, tightly coiled as it was around the rue du Fouarre, crawled with students, professors, artisans and artists. Thomas landed at the right place at the right time. The soil was ready to be plowed.

He began to write and dictate technical discussions, commentaries and summas or summaries of doctrinal questions and answers. The output was awe-inspiring, rigorous and voluminous—so voluminous that the critical Latin edition of his *opera omnia* commissioned by Pope Leo XIII in 1879, well over a hundred years ago, has kept scholars busy into our times and has yet to be completed.

As tradition has it, on December 6, 1273, Thomas celebrated mass and then suddenly abandoned his usual routine, refusing to write or dictate anything else. Had he had a divine vision, a stroke, a mental breakdown or a change of heart? His companion, Reginald of Piperno, urged him to return to his work, but Thomas simply replied, "Reginald, I cannot, because all that I have written seems like straw to me."[16] He died three months later on March 7, 1274.

Much of what we think we know about God is surely straw, if not weeds. And yet, God has seen fit to make use of our straw-filled heads. Indeed, in Christ, God desires that we *do* come to knowledge about him—or rather we should say, that we *know* him. We were made for relationship. Aquinas struggled to find the proper way for humans to talk about God and about our relationship with him. Ultimately he believed that the best way was not affirmative or negative, univocal or equivocal, but *analogical.* "We cannot grasp what God is, but what He is not, and the relation other things have with Him."[17] We can talk about God in terms of the relation God enjoys with other things—by comparison with other things, which is to say, by analogy. All words used to express God's nature and actions are at best analogies, limited attempts to put in words what cannot by definition *be* put in words. We speak most truthfully and reverently when we say "God is *like*—" or "God is *unlike*—."

In contrast to someone like Duns Scotus, Aquinas argues that when we say the world exists and God exists, we are using "exists" in two different but related ways.[18] The world exists *as* God's creation; God exists as its Creator. The world has a beginning and an end; God has neither. We say "God exists" because we have no better words to express the truth of the matter. But we must recognize we speak of God's existence only as an analogy to our existence; God exists *like* we exist, only completely differently. In fact, it is more proper to say our existence is analogical to God's existence, not the other way around; we exist only insofar as God exists all the more.[19]

---

[16]Brian Davies, *The Thought of Thomas Aquinas* (New York: Oxford University Press, 1992), p. 9.
[17]Thomas Aquinas *Contra Gentiles* 1.30.
[18]Thomas Aquinas *De Potentia* 7.2.
[19]Anselm of Canterbury articulates the difference in the *Monologion.* Of God's existence "it is correctly said to be without qualification, absolutely and perfectly. As for all other things, it is correct to deny that they exist absolutely perfectly, and without qualification. . . . They exist in a

Let there be no misunderstanding: analogies, metaphors and comparisons are not attempts to dilute the faith or compromise God's character. By suggesting that we speak analogically, Aquinas is not trying to blur God's identity or reduce theology to putty that could be stretched and conformed to fit any religion or experience ("God is like *this* and *that* and *anything* and *everything!*"). He quotes the ever-prudent St. Jerome as saying, "Careless words involve risk of heresy."[20] Analogy presents itself as a way to *increase* theological precision, not decrease it. Analogy guards spiritual humility and returns theology to its biblical roots.

To see the advantage of analogy and to see how an analogical understanding of language can be put to work, let us take an example from St. Thomas Aquinas and adapt it for our use. Consider how the word "wise" is used in these two statements.

Adam English is wise.

God is wise.

Is "wise" being used in the same way in both statements? We should hope to God not! If we were to claim so, we might be dealing with a case of blasphemy. God's wisdom and human wisdom are not equivalent. The way of the Lord is mysterious; divine wisdom absorbs and explodes all human attempts at wisdom. "The foolishness of God is wiser than man's wisdom" (1 Cor 1:25). It is not that God simply has infinitely more wisdom than me or my wife or Billy Graham or the Pope, God has an irreconcilably different *kind* of wisdom.[21] "Where can wisdom be found? Where does understanding dwell?" (Job 28:12). The difference between human and divine wisdom is not quantitative so much as it is qualitative. Our wisdom perceives and understands, God's wisdom causes, vivifies and makes happen. Francis Bacon once observed, "God is only self-like, having nothing in common with any creature, otherwise than as in shadow and trope."[22]

---

changeable way: in some respect they now are not what they were, or will be, and are what they have not been, or will not be" (Anselm *Monologion* 28, in *The Major Works*, ed. Brian Davies and G. R. Evans [New York: Oxford University Press, 1998], p. 44).

[20]Thomas Aquinas *Summa Theologiae* Ia, Q.39, A.7, obj. 1.

[21]Thomas Aquinas *Summa Theologiae* 1a, Q.13, A.12; also see Placher, *Domestication of Transcendence*, pp. 29, 31.

[22]Francis Bacon, quoted in Soskice, *Metaphor*, p. 63.

Wise in "God is wise" is best understood as neither univocal nor equivocal. We are not saying God is *not* wise, of course, but neither do we want to say we know exactly how wise God is. *Wise* is used by way of comparison, to express what God is like and unlike. And so, Aquinas patiently explains, "analogy is that form of discourse that is apophatic and cataphatic at once."[23] Analogies are somewhere in between yes and no, somewhere in between an affirmation and a negation.

What kind of connections do analogies make, then?

Let's think about another example from Aquinas: the word *healthy*. Consider a healthy person, a healthy diet, a healthy appetite and a healthy complexion.[24] *Healthy* means something different in each usage—a healthy diet might interfere with the growlings of a healthy appetite and a healthy complexion does not necessarily indicate a healthy person. Despite the differences, the word is the same, and so there must be *some* connection. But it is hard to say exactly *what* that connection is. The usage is neither univocal nor equivocal, it is analogical. A healthy person is *like* a healthy diet and a healthy appetite is *like* a healthy complexion . . . but different, of course.

A generation after Aquinas's demise, Duns Scotus crossed the channel and traveled south to Paris—still the intellectual nerve center of Europe—to put forward the argument, with all due respect to the former master, that the most important statements we can make about God are affirmative and definitive, as in "God exists" (which, as we noted, he understood to be a univocal statement). Aquinas would not have been impressed by Duns Scotus's flashy arguments. True to Scripture, he recognized that the most important revelations of God in Scripture are analogical: as a strong fortress, a faithful husband, a hen hovering over her chicks, a dove descending, a king, a shepherd. These are similitudes, comparisons, parables, metaphors. Someone might protest and assert that the Bible does not speak analogically, "Isn't God *literally* the father of all things, and doesn't calling it 'just an analogy' compromise God's fatherhood?" Thomas Aquinas might respond:

---

[23]David B. Hart, *The Beauty of the Infinite* (Grand Rapids: Eerdmans, 2003), p. 306.
[24]Thomas Aquinas *Summa Theologiae* 1a, Q.13, A,10; also see Placher, *Domestication of Transcendence*, p. 28.

Does God have facial hair and male genitalia? Of course not. "God is spirit, and his worshipers must worship in spirit and truth" (Jn 4:24). Conjectures about God's masculine body parts miss the point of calling God "Father." Our clear-sighted Dominican instructor says,

> It is befitting Holy Scripture to put forward divine and spiritual truths by means of comparisons with material things. For God provides for everything according to the capacity of its nature. Now it is natural to man to attain to intellectual truths through sensible things, because all our knowledge originates from sense. Hence in Holy Scripture spiritual truths are fittingly taught under the likeness of material things . . . . It is also befitting Holy Scripture, which is proposed to all without distinction of persons—To the wise and to the unwise I am a debtor (Rom 1:14)—that spiritual truths be expounded by means of figures taken from corporeal things, in order that thereby even the simple who are unable by themselves to grasp intellectual things may be able to understand it.[25]

Further he says, "similitudes drawn from things farthest away from God form within us a truer estimate that God is above whatsoever we may say or think of Him."[26] It may be with this Thomistic truth in mind that David Bentley Hart says in his magisterial book *The Beauty of the Infinite* that the use of theological analogies "'clarifies' language about God not by reducing it to principles of simple similitude, but by making it more complex, more abundant and polyphonic, richer, deeper, fuller, according to the grammar of praise; it offers all words back up to the Word, who sets them free."[27]

Similitudes and comparisons remind us of the limits of our language. They keep us humble. "You save the humble, but your eyes are on the haughty to bring them low" (2 Sam 22:28). Not only are our minds and our linguistic abilities naturally limited, they are unnaturally darkened and plagued by sin with the result that we cannot find, know or appreciate God on our own. Knowledge of God must be revealed. We must be told, shown and invited. "Blessed are those who are invited to the

---

[25]Thomas Aquinas *Summa Theologiae* 1a, Q.1, A.9.

[26]Ibid.

[27]Hart, *Beauty of the Infinite*, p. 310. Also see Nicholas Lash, *Theology on the Way to Emmaus* (London: SCM Press, 1986), p. 109; Brian Wicker, *The Story-Shaped World* (London: Athlone, 1975), pp. 2-27.

wedding supper of the Lamb" (Rev 19:9). The direction of revelation is from heaven to earth. "The bread of God is he who comes down from heaven and gives life to the world" (Jn 6:33).

PRACTICING WHAT WE SPEAK

The discussion of analogies might be understood as a basic grammar lesson. When speaking God-talk, it is important to follow certain rules and pay attention to certain features of the language. That is to say, in a sense, speaking of God requires its own dialect. But what is this new tongue and what is it called? The name of the Christian dialect is *Trinity*. Trinity is more than *what* Christians name God, it is *how* Christians name God. More accurately, it is how God names himself in and through Jesus Christ and how God directs us to address him. God is named by "Father, Son and Holy Spirit." To the question, "What are you talking about?" the Christian answers, "God. God is *what* we are talking about." To the question, "And *how* do Christians talk about their God?" the answer is, "We talk about God using the words revealed in Scripture: Father, Son and Spirit. That is *how* we refer to and address God." Different religions talk about things divine in different ways; for Christians, the word "God" names the One who is Three. To again make ourselves clear, it is not that we have chosen to call God Three in One; God has chosen to reveal his threefold nature to us—Father, Son and Spirit.

Trinity does not represent some *fact* that can be learned from an index card about God like the circumference of the globe or the names of U.S. presidents. Trinity designates how Christians express, worship and relate to God. In the same way, *¡Hola!* does not *mean* "hello" in Spanish as much as it is *how* you say hello in Spanish. Thomas Aquinas emphatically declares, "The Christian faith consists above all in the confession of the Holy Trinity, and it glories especially in the cross of our Lord Jesus Christ."[28] This is who God is and who he has shown himself to be. The Christian faith consists in speaking trinitarianly.

---

[28]Thomas Aquinas *De articulis fidei et ecclesiae sacramentis, ad Archiepiscopum Panormintanum,* quoted in Fergus Kerr, *After Aquinas* (Malden, Mass.: Blackwell, 2002), p. 162. Kerr points out that Thomas made this remark on "the articles of faith" around 1265, just before beginning his *Summa Theologiae.*

The biblical warrant for trinitarian language is rich and plentiful.

- "Therefore go and make disciples of all nations, baptizing them in the name of the Father and of the Son and of the Holy Spirit" (Mt 28:19).

- Jesus says, "All that belongs to the Father is mine. That is why I said the Spirit will take from what is mine and make it known to you" (Jn 16:15).

- About Jesus it is said, "Exalted to the right hand of God, he has received from the Father the promised Holy Spirit and has poured out what you now see and hear" (Acts 2:33).

- About the Spirit, "The Spirit searches all things, even the deep things of God. For who among men knows the thoughts of a man except the man's spirit within him? In the same way, no one knows the thoughts of God except the Spirit of God" (1 Cor 2:10-11).

- About the Father, "There is but one God, the Father, from whom all things came and for whom we live; and there is but one Lord, Jesus Christ, through whom all things came and through whom we live" (1 Cor 8:6).

- About the Trinity, "May the grace of the Lord Jesus Christ and the love of God and the fellowship of the Holy Spirit be with you all" (2 Cor 13:14).

- "Grace to you and peace from God our Father and the Lord Jesus Christ" (Philem 1:3).

- "And our fellowship is with the Father and with his Son, Jesus Christ. . . . We are from God, and whoever knows God listens to us; but whoever is not from God does not listen to us. This is how we recognize the Spirit of truth and the spirit of falsehood" (1 Jn 1:3; 4:6).

These passages represent only a sample of a much greater body of textual evidence. The witness of the biblical text seems to indicate that we do not start with the idea of a being called God, and then add on as an afterthought the idea that this God is triune, three in one. Rather, the most basic language Scripture offers to speak of God is itself trinitarian. The word *Trinity* does not appear in the pages of the Bible because *Trinity* is not a theory the Bible puts forward about God. *Trinity* names the language of the Bible. The Bible speaks fluent trinitarianism the way I speak fluent English—naturally and without preamble or justification.

I would argue there is no way to understand Jesus, his person, his mission and his ministry, without reckoning the Trinity. As the eminent Wabash professor William Placher (1948–2008) suggests, "If . . . we can know God only as revealed in Christ through the Holy Spirit, then we *start* with three."[29] To start with Jesus (as orthodox and evangelical Christians rightly insist on doing) is to start with God the Father, God the Son and God the Spirit. That is to say, Father, Son and Spirit are not "just" names; they identify who God is in himself, who God is in Jesus Christ and who God is for us. Later in the same book Placher reiterates, "Christians start knowing God in God's self-revelation in Jesus Christ, in Jesus' references to the one he called 'Father,' and in the Holy Spirit, the *Paraclete* Jesus promised, who forms and sustains our faith."[30]

Nevertheless, many believers remain very skittish when it comes to God as Father, Son and Spirit. Most are so unsure about what to make of the Trinity that they do not bother with it. The literary giant Dorothy L. Sayers famously observed that for the average pew dweller, "The Father is incomprehensible, the Son is incomprehensible, and the whole thing is incomprehensible. Something put in by theologians to make it more difficult."[31] I suspect the source of much anxiety and neglect with regards to the Trinity comes from a confusion between the "what" and the "how." There is a prevailing assumption that the idea of Trinity communicates some "what," some fact about God's personality, some paradoxical information about God.

We are left scratching our collective heads: How can three equal one? 3 = 1? Pastors concoct all manner of clever explanations to clarify

---

[29]William Placher, *The Triune God* (Louisville, Ky.: Westminster John Knox, 2007), p. 1, emphasis his.
[30]Ibid., p. 120.
[31]Dorothy L. Sayers, *Creed or Chaos?* (New York: Harcourt, Brace, 1949), p. 22.

the mathematical mystery. Just as H_2O can materialize in three different states—liquid, gas and solid—so God persists in three different
states—Father, Son and Spirit. Or, think about the first, middle and
last name of an individual; the three petals of the Irish shamrock; the
root, shoot and fruit of a plant; the one sun, which can be experienced
as light, heat or as a physical object far off in space. These analogies
each have value in helping our minds think about threeness and oneness. But they all seem to miss the point of trinitarian language: God
the Father, Son and Spirit are not names for three individual entities,
beings or substances in God; instead, they name relationships. The *relations* between the three *are* the substance. Augustine elucidates, "when
you say 'being' [with reference to the Trinity] you point not to being but
to relationship."[32] It is not that the language of Father, Son and Spirit
locates three individual members of the Trinity, but rather the relations
implied in the names constitute trinitarian language.

It is like the word *parenthood*. *Parenthood* is a noun (as opposed to a
verb or an adjective), but it does not exactly identify an individual; it
indicates a *relationship* between certain individuals. Father and mother
enjoy the relationship of parenthood with their children. The relationship is what *parenthood* means. So in the Trinity the Father is father by
virtue of begetting and sending the Son, and the Son is son only insofar
as he receives his being and identity from the Father, and the Spirit is
not just some random extra, but the breath of God, the will of the Father and the presence of the Son. The relationships are what Trinity
means; Trinity is the language of relationship.

If these three relationships make up God's one being, why do we
refer to them as three "persons" as in the popular hymn, "Holy, holy,
holy, merciful and mighty! God in three Persons, blessed Trinity"?
Speaking of three persons seems to confuse things because it implies
three personalities, three wills, memories, beings. Augustine expresses
his own dissatisfaction with the limits of language at this point. He
admits that *persons* does not exactly capture what we intend in prayer,
what we know from Scripture and what we believe by faith. He makes

---

[32]Augustine *The Trinity* 7.2, trans. Edmund Hill (Brooklyn, N.Y.: New City Press, 1991),
    p. 219.

clear that "if three persons, then what is meant by person is common to all three."[33] In other words, we must understand *person* not in terms of individuality but in terms of *commonality*, in terms of relationship. Augustine admits that when we declare that God is three in one, we have to give some kind of answer when asked, "Three what?"[34] Divinities? Entities? Beings? Parts? Modes? Bodies? Forms? Types? Persons? "Persons" might be the worst answer we could give . . . except for all the other answers we could give! *Persons* is better than *beings* or *parts* or even *modes*. Augustine shrugs his shoulders at the limits of language and concludes that "three persons" is the traditional and perhaps the best answer we can give to the question "Three what?"

Over eight hundred years later, Thomas Aquinas picked up Augustine's train of thought and added that the three persons in the Trinity are not three separate individual beings or three mini-gods, rather, "this term person signifies in God a relation as subsisting in the divine nature."[35] "God in three persons" describes not only God's relationship to humanity, but most fundamentally, what Father, Son and Spirit share in common. It describes how God himself is constituted. *Father* signifies an eternally subsisting relation with the Son, *Son* signifies a persisting relation with the Father, and *Holy Spirit* signifies the spirit of Father and Son, the relational presence of God. The personhood of the Father, the Son and the Spirit are *real*, not nominal or "merely" relational. Indeed, the oneness of God is founded upon a unity of divine persons. The Trinity is a triunity of divine persons.[36]

Given the present discussion, some theologians have suggested that it might be more accurate to refer to the Trinity not in terms of three persons but "personal relationships" or "three person-constituting relations."[37]

---

[33]Ibid., 7.8, p. 226.

[34]Ibid., 7.7, p. 225.

[35]Thomas Aquinas *Summa Theologiae* 1.30.1; also see the two articles following article 30 and 1.29.4.

[36]Thanks to Gary Deddo for this clarification.

[37]Paul Fiddes, *Participating in God* (Louisville, Ky.: Westminster John Knox, 2001), p. 49; Gerald O'Collins, *The Tripersonal God* (New York: Paulist Press, 1999), p. 179. O'Collins explains "person-constituting relations" this way: "in the Trinity there are three person-constituting relations: generating, being generated, 'being spirated'—and a fourth, nonperson-constituting relation, the active spiration of the Spirit as a common peculiarity of the Father and the Son, something that belongs to the Son as deriving from the Father."

These and other suggestions have the advantage of precision, but I worry that many of them are reductionistic. The more elaborate the definition, the greater the tendency to think that Father, Son and Spirit are "just" names or that they are "merely" relationships and nothing more. Instead of forcing the language to fit, I would prefer to say: here is where the wheels fall off of our language. *We worship the God revealed in three persons.* There is a right and proper mystery about what exactly it means to say this. No word, no analogy, no definition, no metaphor suffices to explain it. God has graciously bent low enough for us to see him, but that does not mean that we should expect our finite words and thoughts to capture his infinite wonder and capricious pleasure.

The triune God of the Holy Scripture is the God who exists totally in community, who is defined by relationship and who gives and receives in intimate and eternal fellowship of the three. Stephen Long explains in practical terms what this means:

> It means God is not like us, for we are not constituted entirely by our relations. No matter how much I seek to give myself to my wife, my children, my friends, I cannot give myself to them in the same way that the Triune Persons give themselves to each other.[38]

But there is more. Because God is relational, defined by the giving and receiving that is the Trinity, our Lord reveals his relational nature in relationship with us. "No one comes to the Father except through me" (Jn 14:6). God the Father is God over us; God the Son is God come to us; God the Spirit is God with us; God the Trinity is God *for us.* Irenaeus declares, "The Father is indeed above all, and He is the Head of Christ; but the Word is through all things, and is Himself the Head of the Church; while the Spirit is in us all, and He is the living water."[39] From a pastoral point of view, *Trinity* expresses in shorthand the fact that God is for us, cares about us like a good father, desires relationship with us like a good brother or son, walks with us and guides our spirit. Not only does each member of the Trinity relate to

---

[38]Stephen Long, "God Is Not Nice," *God Is Not . . .* , ed. Brent Laytham (Grand Rapids: Brazos, 2004), p. 51.

[39]Irenaeus *Against Heresies* 5.28, ANF, vol. 1, p. 546.

and co-inhere with the other members in the Godhead, each member relates to *us*. We are the Father's creation, the Son's handiwork and the Spirit's beloved.

In the final analysis, the Trinity is mysterious. But the mystery is not: "How can 3 = 1? How can three persons equal one God?" The enigma is not mathematical. If we stop there, then we completely miss the real mystery. The real question is: *Why did God the Father, Son and Spirit—the perfect community of eternal divinity, not abandon us rebellious and pitiful humans to our sin and self-destruction?* Discovering God in three persons means discovering that *God has not abandoned us*. God has not walked away from his creation, even when it tried to tear itself away. Instead, the God who fathered the universe by giving it form and life chose to come into the world as a mere human, with all the trappings of gender, race, sweat and blood. In accepting the conditions of human life, the incarnate Son also accepted a cruel human death for the forgiveness of sins. Why would God do this? The Spirit answers: *that is the mystery that is the Trinity.*

CHRISTIANITY AS LANGUAGE

MAKING SUBSTITUTIONS

TIM CONDER, THE EVANGELICALLY MINDED pastor of a wonderful emergent church community in Durham, North Carolina, known as Emmaus Way, once received "a blistering critique" in response to a series of talks he delivered. A young graduate student who had heard the talks accused Conder of misrepresenting the gospel because he had told the audience to "define their lives by Jesus' story" and "seek the face of God." After repeating Conder's words back to him, the student added, "Whatever that means!"

Conder later reflected that the roadblock he encountered with his young critic had not been one of doctrine as much as language. "I didn't use the theological language favored by this student; therefore my points were frivolous, obtuse, or even scandalous."[1] Using the "right" words or the "wrong" words can make all the difference. Words can confuse or clarify, destroy or defend, alienate or allay. No wonder James 3:1-12 warns teachers to watch what they say and tame their tongues as best they can.

As we saw in the last chapter, trinitarian language does not serve the purpose of mechanical logicians, nor does it outline in rigid terms "what" God is composed of; the language of Father, Son and Spirit is the language of prayer, preaching and the Bible—it announces a holy revelation. Trinity is not only "who" God is but "how" God reveals

---

[1]Tim Conder, *The Church in Transition* (Grand Rapids: Zondervan, 2006), p. 149.

himself. Paul Fiddes, former Principal of Regent's Park College, Oxford University, says the idiom of the Trinity is not intended only for making observations about God, but for *participation* in the life of God.[2] It is *how* the Son has taught us through the Spirit to relate to and worship the Father.

Fiddes makes the theological observation that we do not pray *to* relationships as much as we pray *in* relationship. We pray *to* God our Father, *in* the strong name of Jesus Christ, *through* the power and guidance of the Holy Spirit. Likewise, when a believer makes the sign of the cross in the name of the Father, Son and Holy Spirit, she sweeps her finger downward portraying the movement of the Father to the Son and then vertically across her chest reminding us that the Spirit is always opening new horizons and broadening our relationship with God. Other churches regularly sing the Doxology upon collecting the tithes and offerings. This is a trinitarian practice ending with, "Praise Him above ye heavenly host, Praise Father, Son, and Holy Ghost." Baptism in the name of the Father, the Son and the Holy Spirit, as Matthew 28 commands, stirs deeply trinitarian waters. Fiddes pens this beautiful description of the baptismal event:

> Being plunged beneath the waters which represent the hostile forces of death and chaos (Ps. 18:15-17), the baptismal candidate shares in the mission of the Son who is sent by the Father to be immersed into the bitterness and alienation of death; emerging from the water, raised with Christ to new life (Rom 6:4), the believer is taken up into the breath of the Spirit who opens new possibilities even in the waters of death, turning it into life-giving water so that she is born again of water and the spirit. This is baptism *into* the triune name, *into* movements whose direction is shown by the names.[3]

MAKING SUBSTITUTIONS

The family resemblance between language systems and Christian belief is strong. As has been shown, the "language" spoken by the Chris-

---

[2]Paul Fiddes, *Participating in God* (Louisville, Ky.: Westminster John Knox, 2001), p. 41.
[3]Ibid., p. 44. Also see David B. Hart, *The Beauty of the Infinite* (Grand Rapids: Eerdmans, 2003), p. 168.

tian is "trinitarian." Trinity provides the vocabulary and the grammar for Christian theology and worship. Now let's give a twist to the comparison. It often happens that one word substitutes for another. With nicknames, synonyms, translations or updates, things get renamed. So the question is: are Father, Son and Holy Spirit essential and eternal names for God? Or, can those names be replaced with others?

It is not as crazy as it sounds. A number of important theologians, especially those with a keen eye for gender equality, have challenged the traditional language of the Trinity as being overly weighted toward the masculine. Elizabeth Johnson, in her provocative and award-winning book *She Who Is*, asks the simple question:

> But what results when the human reality used to point to God is always and everywhere male? The sacred character of maleness is revealed, while femaleness is relegated to the unholy darkness without. . . . The patriarchal symbol of the divine sculpts men into the role of God, fully in "his" image and capable of representing "him," while women, thought to be only deficiently in the image of God, and ultimately a symbol of evil, play the role of dependent and sinful humanity who when forgiven may then be recipients of grace or spiritual helpers. No one has yet summed up more pithily the total sociological and theological fallout of androcentric symbolism for the divine than Mary Daly with her apothegm "if God is male, then the male is God."[4]

Thoughtlessly equating God with masculinity tends to promote patriarchal systems and marginalize women. To show how comfortable we have become with masculine imagery for God, Johnson points out that no one raises an eyebrow when images of God as father, king, lord, bridegroom and husband are used in worship, but there is dismay and protest if even a single contrasting feminine image is spoken—like God as mother, wife or queen. "If it is not meant that God is male when masculine imagery is used, why the objection when female images are introduced?"[5]

---

[4]Elizabeth Johnson, *She Who Is* (New York: Crossroad, 1996), p. 37.
[5]Ibid., p. 34. Also see Joy Ann McDougall, "Keeping Feminist Faith with Christian Tradition," *Modern Theology* 24, no. 1 (2008): 103-124; Teresa Berger, "The Challenge of Gender for Liturgical Tradition," *Worship* 82, no. 3 (2008): 243-61.

Johnson recommends that, with all deference to the biblical language and the historical Christian tradition, perhaps new trinitarian images are in order—images that are overtly feminine. Only so would Christians be able to dislodge deep-seated masculine views of God. "At this point in the living tradition I believe that we need a strong dose of explicitly female imagery to break the unconscious sway that male trinitarian imagery holds over the imaginations of even the most sophisticated thinking."[6] For her part, she suggests Sophia-Spirit, Sophia-Jesus and Sophia-Mother (*Sophia* is the Greek word for wisdom and is usually associated with the feminine divine).

Johnson is not the first to suggest this alternative scheme. As early as the second century A.D., a group known to us as the Valentinian Gnostics also made use of the feminine Sophia to represent divine will and activity. According to Irenaeus, the church father who relates the story, the Valentinians said that somewhere in the recesses of time something tragic happened to Sophia, who was the emanation of divine wisdom. She gave birth to a malformed and unworkable glob of matter we call earth. The material world thus came from the womb of Sophia and so shares in her wisdom and order but also in the grief and deformity of her miscarriage.[7] I raise the example of the Valentinian Gnostics to call attention to the fact that even as Elizabeth Johnson attempts to play a new anthem for the Trinity in a feminist key, she uses preexisting notes: in this case, the language of "Sophia." When she depicts the Trinity in terms of Sophia, she has not freed herself from the burden of fatherhood and sonship language as much as she has adopted the burden of Sophia language, which has its own history and baggage. And now, as often as she uses it, she must add, "When I use the term 'Sophia' I don't mean that God is a woman . . ." Isn't this what theologians must already do with fatherhood language: "When I use the term 'Father' I don't mean that God is a man . . ."?

Johnson's reconfiguration of the Trinity is just one among many. Other modern theologians have bravely pushed forward their own sub-

---

[6]Johnson, *She Who Is*, p. 212.
[7]Irenaeus *Against Heresies* 4.1, ANF, vol. 1, pp. 320-21.

stitutions for traditional trinitarian language.[8]

- Langdon Gilkey interprets the holy Trinity as divine Being, divine Logos, divine Love[9]
- Peter Hodgson: the One (Father) who Loves (Son) in Freedom (Spirit)[10]
- John Macquarrie: primordial Being, expressive Being and unitive Being[11]
- Sallie McFague: Mother, Lover and Friend of the world[12]
- Heribert Mühlen: the I, Thou and We of love[13]
- Raimundo Panikkar: Source, Being and Return to being[14]
- Letty Russell: Creator, Liberator and Advocate[15]
- Stephen Webb: Giver, Given and Giving[16]

New and creative expressions of the faith are always welcome and even necessary for the vitality of the living church. However, one overarching and obvious dilemma remains: any renaming goes against God's own self revelation. Father, Son and Spirit is how God has revealed himself and how God has named himself.

There is another reason to advise caution replacing Father, Son and Spirit with substitutions of our own invention: changing words changes meaning and changing the meaning changes the language. It has a snowball effect. Of course, words are always changing and being changed. New editions of dictionaries are always dropping

---

[8]For survey treatment, see Robert Letham, *The Holy Trinity: In Scripture, History, Theology, and Worship* (Phillipsburg, N.J.: P & R, 2004); Roger Olson and Christopher Hall, *The Trinity* (Grand Rapids: Eerdmans, 2002); Johnson, *She Who Is*, p. 210.

[9]Langdon Gilkey, *Message and Existence: An Introduction to Christian Theology* (New York: Seabury, 1980).

[10]Peter Hodgson, *Winds of the Spirit* (Louisville, Ky.: Westminster John Knox Press, 1994).

[11]John Macquarrie, *Principles of Christian Theology* (New York: Charles Scribner's Sons, 1966).

[12]Sallie McFague, *The Body of God: An Ecological Theology* (Minneapolis: Fortress, 1993).

[13]Heribert Mühlen, *Der heilige Geist als Person*, 2nd ed. (Münster: Aschendorff, 1966).

[14]Raimundo Panikkar, *The Cosmotheandric Experience: Emerging Religious Consciousness* (Maryknoll, N.Y.: Orbis, 1986).

[15]Letty Russell, *Household of Freedom: Authority in Feminist Theology* (Philadelphia: Westminster Press, 1979).

[16]Stephen Webb, *The Gifting God* (New York: Oxford University Press, 1996).

words that have gone out of use and adding new ones that have come into vogue. Substitutions in language happen for all sorts of reasons. But changes affect more than just the word in question, they affect the entire language. With enough minor alterations, one language becomes another. Compare the Middle English of Chaucer's fourteenth-century masterpiece, *The Canterbury Tales*, with the contemporary English of any present-day novelist. For many readers, it is hard to recognize Chaucer's archaic forms, spellings and expressions *as English*. Many contemporary readers in fact read Chaucer *in translation*—from the English of one era to the English of another. A few small and seemingly insignificant changes to words add up to big changes to a language; so also a few changes to our words about God add up.

Is something the same if its name is changed? How much change needs to occur before one thing becomes something else? The celebrated Greek historian Plutarch, who lived in the first century A.D., recounts the plight of an historic ship that underwent a complete replacement of its parts:

> The ship wherein Theseus and the youth of Athens returned had thirty oars, and was preserved by the Athenians down even to the time of Demetrus Phalereus, for they took away the old planks as they decayed, putting in new and stronger timber in their place, insomuch as this ship became a standing example among the philosophers for the logical question as to things that grow; one side holding that the ship remained the same, and the other contending it was not the same.[17]

Philosopher Roy Sorensen notes a case from more recent times: the story of the London Bridge. Built in 1831, it was auctioned off by the British government in the 1960s to an American entrepreneur, Robert McCulloch. McCulloch dismantled and reassembled the bridge in a city in Arizona that he himself founded, Lake Havasu City. The big question is: Is the transported and reassembled bridge really the London Bridge if it resides in Arizona and not London? Is the Athenian

---

[17]Plutarch, *Plutarch's Lives of Illustrious Men*, quoted in Roy Sorensen, *A Brief History of the Paradox* (New York: Oxford University Press, 2003), p. 132.

ship really the ship of Theseus if all its original planks and boards have been replaced by new ones?[18]

What might result from substituting one name for God with another or trading the traditional members of the Trinity for different ones? Actually, a substitution for God's name has been tried once before—in biblical times no less.

In Exodus 3 the Architect of the Universe gives to Moses his personal name. It comes as a response to Moses' own request. Moses encounters a deity who speaks fire from a bush on Mount Horeb and identifies himself as the god of Moses' ancestors. Moses is commanded to return to Egypt to liberate the descendents of those ancestors. But Moses is not so sure. Bowing in a sweat before the flaming bush, he says, "Suppose I go to the Israelites and say to them, 'The God of your fathers has sent me to you,' and they ask me, 'What is his name?' what shall I tell them?" (Ex 3:13). It is an understandable but completely audacious request. If the Lord refused to give his name to Jacob at the ford of the Jabbok, "Why do you ask my name?" (Gen 32:29) as he would later do to Samson's parents, "Why do you ask my name? It is beyond understanding" (Judg 13:18), what can Moses have realistically expected? Who does he think he is?

Surpassing all expectations, God responds to Moses, "I AM WHO I AM" and then adds, "This is what you are to say to the Israelites, 'I AM has sent me to you'" (Ex 3:14). The Hebrew word here for the divine name is יהוה and is transliterated with English letters as YHWH. Originally, Hebrew script used no vowels, only consonants, as I have represented it here. Vowel pointings were added much later to help readers pronounce the words.

An odd thing happened somewhere along the way. As devout Jews read the sacred Hebrew texts in synagogue worship, they began the practice of *not* pronouncing יהוה.[19] To them it seemed disrespectful, arrogant and out of place to call by his first name the Holy One who shakes out the corners of the earth like a garment, as if he were no more

---

[18]See Sorensen, *A Brief History of the Paradox*, p. 133.
[19]See Bruce Metzger, "To the Reader," *The New Oxford Annotated Bible*, NRSV, 3rd ed. (New York: Oxford University Press, 2007), p. xx.

than a buddy. Surely the almighty Maker of heaven and earth deserves a bit more reverence, right? So when Jewish readers would come to this word in the text, they would say *Adonai*, Hebrew for "Lord" or "Master," instead of יהוה (YHWH).[20] In effect, they were saying, Mr. God, thank you very much. They made a substitution: a respectful title for a personal name.

To help readers remember not to utter the holy name, the Hebrew scribes, or Masoretes, put the vowel markings for Adonai underneath YHWH. The reader would come to the word, and immediately recognize that the vowel indicators were incorrect for that type of word, and then remember to say Adonai. Later translators unfamiliar with the history were baffled by this apparent mistake in the Hebrew. They could tell that the vowel pointings did not match up with the consonants. But what could they do? They trusted the text and simply joined the consonants YHWH with the out-of-place vowel pointings, a, o, ai, and came up with a whole new word, "Jehovah." This new name is used seven times in the King James 1611 Authorized Version of Bible. It also appears in many older hymns, sermons and is the preferred translation of YHWH in the 1901 American Standard Version of the Bible. "Jehovah" is a great attempt to clean up a linguistic mess, but it most certainly does not represent how Moses and the ancient Israelites pronounced the holy name.

Do contemporary scholars know how the divine name was originally pronounced? Not with certainty. Its pronunciation was so completely avoided and for so long substituted, again out of reverence and awe, that eventually no one remembered how it should be said. Nevertheless, following the rules of pronunciation, the Hebrew word יהוה should probably be said "Yahweh."[21]

Where does all of this leave modern translators of the Bible? There are many options as to how to translate this word: "Yahweh," "Lord," "Adonai," "Jehovah" or simply "YHWH." The common consensus is to

---

[20] The Greek translators followed suite by using the word *Kyrios* ("Lord") as did the Latins with *Dominus* ("Lord"). Ibid.

[21] At any rate, this is how the word is now pronounced even in pop culture. For example, the Grammy-winning Irish rock band U2 recorded a song by the title "Yahweh" on their album *How to Dismantle an Atomic Bomb*.

split the difference and render the divine name as "LORD," small caps. When you see "LORD" in the biblical text, it indicates that the Hebrew word יהוה is being used: the personal name of God.

The question to be asked from this long and involved history is: Does God become more revered and awesome when held at a greater distance? Does the practice of *not* saying Yahweh make the word that much holier? Does substituting a personal name Yahweh with a formal title Adonai aid in worship and theology and the experience of God? As the history shows, replacing Yahweh with Adonai did not make the personal name of God holier and more revered; it made people forget how to say it!

Contrary to the romantic myth, distance does not make the heart grow fonder, distance makes the heart forget. Long distance relationships do not work, at least not over the long haul. Pushing God farther and farther out does not make God greater and more exalted, it makes God less and less relevant. Deference to God can become exaggerated to the point that we assume the deity cannot possibly be concerned with ordinary problems and really shouldn't be bothered with trivial matters. So we stop bothering God with our little questions and minor requests; eventually we stop bothering God for anything.

By a similar application, we can see that trading Father, Son and Spirit for newer, shinier, and more politically correct labels would probably not resolve dissatisfactions. In fact, it may increase them. The task at hand is not to avoid or replace, but to learn to speak better the language we have inherited. Christians need to learn to speak the biblical language of Trinity with greater fluency, nuance and sensitivity.

IS THE FATHER REALLY THE FATHER?

It is Jesus who most thoroughly identifies God as Father. The banner of Christ's message unfurls as *the revelation of the fatherhood of God*. Almost to the exclusion of other names for God, Jesus prays to "our Father in heaven" (Mt 6:9), does "the will of my Father" (Mk 14:36), brings "what my Father has promised" (Lk 24:49) and commends worship of the Father (Jn 4:23). Why does Jesus invoke this name instead of the personal name given to Moses at the blazing bush—the name that is ubiquitous throughout the Old Testament? Why not call God *Yahweh*? By Jesus' day it appears that the name had already fallen out of use. One can assume that any attempt on Jesus' part to reintroduce it would not produce the intended results—that is, reminding the people that God is personal and knowable. If Jesus had insisted on calling God *Yahweh*, he would have only produced shock, dismay, confusion and disgust. Instead, Jesus calls God his Father. Why? Because God truly *is* his Father, the Father of the only begotten Son (Jn 3:16).[22] "This is my Son, whom I love; with him I am well pleased," comes the thunderous announcement from the skies at Jesus' baptism (Mt 3:17; 17:5).[23] Jesus corroborates, "I came from the Father and entered the world" (Jn 16:28).

The relationship between Jesus and God is one of Son and Father. The New Testament is saturated with testimony to this truth. In all four Gospels, in Acts, in the Pauline Epistles, in the General Epistles and in Revelation, the identity and unity of Father and Son are declared, confirmed, witnessed, glorified and honored.[24] Any attempt to cite supporting passages on this point would either be woefully fragmentary or would consume the remainder of the chapter . . . and perhaps the book!

There is one Father of our Lord Jesus Christ (2 Cor 1:3; 11:31; Eph 1:3), and there is one eternally begotten Son of the Father (Mt 16:16; Jn 20:17; Heb 1:2), coeternal with the Spirit (Gen 1:2; Rom 8:9). In his famous debate with Gregory of Nyssa (335–394), Eunomius (d. 393), a prominent leader in the second wave of Arianism after the Council of Nicaea, suggested that perhaps the title Father could be replaced with

---

[22]Thomas F. Torrance, "The Christian Apprehension of God the Father," *Speaking the Christian God*, ed. Alvin Kimel (Grand Rapids: Eerdmans, 1992), p. 121.

[23]Athanasius and the other Nicene fathers are quick to point out that God does not say, "This has now become my son," but rather, "This is my Son"—always and from eternity.

[24]Irenaeus encapsulates the relationship between Father and Son as follows,

> For no one can know the Father, unless through the Word of God, that is, unless by the Son revealing Him; neither can he have knowledge of the Son, unless through the good pleasure of the Father. But the Son performs the good pleasure of the Father; for the Father sends, and the Son is sent, and comes. And His Word knows that His Father is, as far as regards us, invisible and infinite; and since He cannot be declared [by anyone else], He does Himself declare Him to us; and on the other hand, it is the Father alone who knows His own Word. (Irenaeus *Against Heresies* 4.6.3, ANF, vol. 1, p. 468)

something more philosophically satisfying, like "Supreme Absolute Being." *Father* was just too earthy and anthropomorphic for the erudite Eunomius. Gregory, who could be equally erudite, nevertheless reminded Eunomius that the Christian religion did not solely consist of "doctrinal precision" and finely tuned philosophical ideas.[25] The Christian faith is bound to divine revelation. Gregory wanted to remain true to that revelation found in Scripture, and so was obliged to confess that the relationship of Father and Son is constitutive and incontrovertible: "without the Son the Father has neither existence nor name" and vice versa.[26]

Scripture demonstrates conclusively that the Father really is the Father of the Son, but what about the father of us? Is *the* Father *our* father? Is our relationship with God as Father the same as the Son's? To what extent are we children of God? The Son is begotten from eternity (Jn 1:1; 17:5), we were conceived and born in time and space. There is only *one* Son, and yet many offspring of God (Acts 17:29). The prophet Malachi asks, "Have we not all one Father? Did not one God create us?" (Mal 2:10). Paul answers this question in the affirmative, "there is . . . one God and Father of all, who is over all and through all and in all" (Eph 4:4-6; see also 1 Cor 8:6). We are all God's children, red and yellow, black and white—every person of every color, creed, gender and age. God has made us all. But not all recognize God as Father or themselves as his children. Salvation, in part, is just that: coming out of a lie and into the knowledge of *who* we are and *whose* we are. It means being adopted and recognized as an heir and given full-standing membership in the household of God (Gal 4:5-7). It means being given a new name: our true name (Rev 2:17). "Do not suppose that it is a small thing that you are being given. You, a pitiable creature, are receiving the family name of God."[27] John's prologue declares that, "to all who received him, to those who believed in his name, he gave the right to become children of God—children born not of natural descent, nor of human decision or a husband's will, but born of God" (Jn 1:12-13). "How great is the

---

[25]Robert L. Wilken, *Spirit of Early Christian Thought* (New Haven, Conn.: Yale University Press, 2003), p. 239.

[26]Gregory of Nyssa *Contra Eunomius* 2.4, NPNF, 2nd series, vol. 5, p. 105.

[27]Cyril of Jerusalem *Procatechesis* 6, Fathers of the Church, vol. 61, p. 75.

love the Father has lavished on us, that we should be called children of God! And that is what we are!" (1 Jn 3:1). That is what we were created to be. That *is* what we are.

Salvation means being declared children of God, and yet, to return to our main point, our status is not the same as the Son's. He the "first-born over all creation" (Col 1:15), and only he can say, "I and the Father are one" (Jn 10:30). Even though we may call ourselves sons and daughters of the Father and heirs to the promise, we are not children in the same way he is. So how is God our Father as well as his? Cyril of Jerusalem explains to his class of soon-to-be baptized Christians,

> It may be well to say by way of preface that though the name of the Father is one, the power of His operation is manifold. Christ, recognizing this very thing, was careful to say: "I go to my Father, and your Father"; He did not say: "to our Father," but, making a distinction, He first said what was proper to Himself: "to my Father," that is, by nature; then He added: "and your Father," that is, by adoption. For though we have been granted the privilege of saying in our prayers: "Our Father who art in heaven," this proceeds from His loving-kindness. For we do not call Him Father as though we were natural sons of our Father who is in heaven; but, having been translated from servitude to adoption as sons, by the grace of the Father, through Son and Holy Spirit, by His ineffable loving-kindness we are privileged to speak thus.[28]

The full inheritance of our identities as sons and daughters is by translation from servitude to adoption into our eternal family; it is by God's own grace and power that we are able to call him our Father (1 Jn 3:1). What does it mean for us to call God "our Father, who art in heaven"? It means that not only have we been *made* creatures of God, we have been *adopted* as sons and daughters and heirs into God's own house.[29] The fatherhood of God offers us healthy, biblical language. It

---

[28]Cyril of Jerusalem *Catechesis* 7.7, Fathers of the Church, vol. 61, p. 174. "But of Christ only is God Father by nature and not by adoption; and He is Father of men in time, but of Christ before all time" (7.10).

[29]Augustine explains: "God has an only son whom he begat of his own substance. . . . He did not, however, beget us of His own substance, for we are a creature which He did not beget, but made. And so in order to make us the brothers of Christ in his own manner, He adopted us. Accordingly, this manner by which God begat us to be his sons by his word and his grace, although we had already been not born of him but made and established, is called adoption.

brings to mind God's closeness and familial concern. To call God Father expresses the conviction that God wants a personal relationship with us, cares for us and nurtures us *like a good father*. But this is not quite adequate. It is not that God is *like* a father—God is the Father. We can strive to act like fathers and mothers in a godly manner; we can strive to imitate the example God sets as Father, but the analogy does not work the other way around. We don't first define good parenting and then see how God fits that description as Father. Jesus pushes this point time and time again. Those of us who are fathers and mothers should be merciful because the Father is merciful (Lk 6:36), not the other way around. We are to love as the Father has loved the Son, not because God's love is like a father's (Jn 15:9).

Jesus understood that his listeners had all kinds of ideas and impressions about fatherhood; some of them had loving and nurturing fathers, others deadbeat, neglectful, abusive or completely absent dads. The same is true today. This is one reason we cannot start from *our* understanding of fathers and then try to apply those expectations to God. Jesus tells his listeners exactly what kind of father God is:

> Which of you, if his son asks for bread, will give him a stone? Or if he asks for a fish, will give him a snake? If you, then, though you are evil, know how to give good gifts to your children, how much more will your Father in heaven give good gifts to those who ask him! (Mt 7:9-11)

This is a father who cares for his children, gives them good gifts, nourishes them, watches over them and loves them. God is not a father in a masculine or patriarchal or paternal sense, but in a parental sense. This is a father who watches for his wayward child to come home, not with his arms crossed and a stern scowl on his face. Instead, he leaps off the porch and runs to the returning son, wraps him up in an embrace, kisses him, clothes him and throws him a party (Lk 15:11-24). What Jesus highlights is the fact that God's fatherhood is "perfect" (Mt 5:48) whereas our attempts to mother and father our children are not. We

---

Hence John says, He gave them the power to be made sons of God. . . . It is he Whom we have as God, Lord, and Father: God, for we were . . . made by him; Lord, for we are subject to him; Father, for we were born again by his adoption" (*Contra Faustum* 3.3, NPNF, 1st series, vol. 4, p. 160).

know how to procreate but God knows how to parent.

So we see that the direction of the analogy has to be reversed. We have said Christianity is like a story and Christianity is like a language, but we should not say God is like a father. We start with the fatherhood of God, and proceed from there.[30] In the same way that we can say, *God is love,* but not the reverse, *love is God,* so we can say, *the Father models parenthood for us,* but not the reverse, *parenthood models the Father.* Jesus puts it as starkly as possible: "do not call anyone on earth 'father,' for you have one Father, and he is in heaven" (Mt 23:9). The Father in heaven defines to what extent there could possibly be fathers on earth.[31] Ephesians agrees, "For this reason I kneel before the Father, from whom all fatherhood in heaven and on earth derives its name" (Eph 3:14-15).

---

[30]Karl Barth writes, "If we call God Father, it is because he is Father in reality. And the relation between God's Fatherhood and fatherhood among men reverses itself: we do not call God Father because we know what that is; on the contrary, because we know God's Fatherhood we afterwards understand what human fatherhood truly is. The divine truth precedes and grounds the human truth" (from *The Faith of the Church*, quoted in Torrance, "Christian Apprehension," p. 130).

[31]The same logic extends through verses 16-22 of Mt 23.

CHRISTIANITY
AS GAME

9

CHRISTIANITY AS GAME

But what are the things which eye has not seen, ear has not heard,

and which have not so much as dimly dawned upon the human heart?

Whatever they are, they are nobler, I believe, than circus, and both

theatres [the theater and the amphitheater], and every race-course.

TERTULLIAN

IT IS EASY TO FORGET THAT football and Old Maid are both games. One involves twenty-two well-padded athletes chasing an inflated ball across a grassy field, and the other involves two individuals sitting down with a selection of cards in their hands. And yet, something identifies them both as games. Every game—whether cycling or rowing or Chutes and Ladders or Trivial Pursuit or tic-tac-toe or croquet—has four identifying features. Bernard Suits, author of *The Grasshopper: Games, Life, and Utopia*, enumerates these four elements: ends or goals (scoring the most points), means (with a ball and a ten-foot-high hoop), rules (within this time limit and on this court and in this manner) and finally players with sporting attitudes (in other words, players must agree to all the conditions of the game and intend to act upon them).[1]

---

[1]Bernard Suits, *The Grasshopper: Games, Life and Utopia* (Toronto: University of Toronto Press, 1978), pp. 34-35. Also see Shaun H. Heap and Yanis Varoufakis, *Game Theory: A Critical Introduction* (London: Routledge, 1995).

Games only function properly when all four elements are present. The next three chapters will be spent exploring these four elements and how they relate to the practice of Christianity. But quickly we will introduce the four points comparison as follows.

✛ Games must have objectives to be obtained, ways of assessing the play, that is, ways of assigning value to the performance. There must be an *end*, purpose or conclusion to the game. These will vary from game to game: in golf the lowest score wins, in track the shortest time wins, in Spades the most number of tricks wins, in racquetball achieving a certain number of points wins. Likewise, we will show that Christianity has an end, a purpose and a goal. Christian discipleship aims at maturity in Christ, Christian worship aims at pleasing God, and the Christian hope finds its ultimate end in the resurrection and life eternal.

✛ Games require not only ends, but also certain *means*, tools, equipment and boundaries. Bowling, for example, requires properly sized and weighted balls which cannot be replaced by any other balls, say, golf balls or tennis balls. Bowling also requires a certain length of lane and a certain number of pins set up in a pyramidal pattern at the end of the lane. Other games require considerably less equipment: hangman only requires a pencil and paper. Christianity operates with certain indispensable pieces of equipment too—the Bible, Christian community, tradition, lived convictions and the guidance of the Spirit.

✛ In addition to means and equipment, games proceed according to specific *rules* and regulations. Games are ritualized contests, and part of the ritual involves rules. Rules give structure to games, informing players which actions are appropriate and when and how those actions should be performed. A basketball team that waits five minutes after time has expired and then sinks a dozen shots and declares victory would be preposterous. The team must make their points within certain time constraints. The time limitation is a key rule in basketball. Likewise, a giddy card player who happens to pick up a great card can't just slap it down as soon as it comes into his or her hand. Cards are played in turn according to a certain preset order; each player must wait his or her turn. Rules, order and organization are also essential to

Christianity. Christianity is, and should be, an organized religion. Rules, order and procedures are not bad things. "To be against organized religion is like being against organized hospitals."[2] In Christianity, some rules are obvious and well articulated (the Ten Commandments), some are unspoken or just assumed (proper attire for attending a worship service). Sometimes the reason why we do something a certain way is purely practical or traditional (Why start a Sunday service at 11:00 a.m.? Why, in a card game, does the person who is left of the dealer always get to play first?). Sometimes there is a deep spiritual reason (think of the way your church distributes or receives Communion).

✚ Besides these three conditions, games require *players with sporting attitudes*. Without players, board games and beach balls sit idly on the shelves collecting dust. Games don't play themselves, they require participants.[3] And one more qualification: participants must agree to the rules, know how to use the equipment and intend to achieve the proper goals of the game. I have summarized this qualification in the phrase "sporting attitude." Some players knowingly violate the rules, misuse the equipment or throw the game. Whether through ignorance or unsportsmanlike conduct, they can ruin the game for everyone. On the other hand, contestants who are skilled, knowledgeable, competitive and fair can make the game thrilling and enjoyable for all. In the same way, we will show that Christianity also requires participants who are committed to the spirit of discipleship, love and obedience.

✚ Games are self-contained, closed systems. Different elements from different games cannot be mixed and matched. One does not bring hockey sticks to a game of bridge, nor does one bring marbles to a vol-

---

[2]William Cavanaugh, "God Is Not Religious," *God Is Not . . .*, ed. Brent Laytham (Grand Rapids: Brazos Press, 2004), p. 98.

[3]I use the plural *participants* even though some games are solo events: for instance, solitaire, running track alone to beat one's own best time or playing chess against a computer program, like Garry Kasparov against IBM's Deep Blue. Nevertheless, even in these instances, another player or player-substitute is usually implied. You run against your own time or you play against the computer. There might be exceptions, but overall the rule still stands: games require more than one participant. This is a point made strongly by William McClendon, *Ethics*, 2nd ed. (Nashville: Abingdon, 2002), p. 172.

leyball court. The rules of play in Candy Land cannot be superimposed upon a ping-pong contest. Neither can the scoring of golf be translated into the scoring of ice skating. It is not that these actions are "wrong" as much as they are nonsensical; they don't make any sense. They appear out of their element. Each game carries its own set of rules, equipment, goals and expectations. Likewise, the elements of Christianity are self-contained and non-transferrable. Those things that are most crucial to the Christian faith might be out of place elsewhere. Taking care of the needy and the elderly are important ways of enacting Christ's commandment to love, but they don't make much sense in a market economy, where profitability is the highest goal. The Christian commitment to marriage and the prohibition of sex outside the bonds of marriage make sense within the framework of the Bible and a theology of love and fidelity, but, let's admit, they often come across as gibberish to outsiders.

These insights into the basic nature of games help us understand something about the Christian faith: how it operates, what it expects and where it marks its boundaries. I intend to investigate in much more detail these four elements of games and how they relate to Christianity, but before we do so, we should take time to point out five ways in which Christianity is *not* like a game. The analogy of games promises to reward richly, but it is not perfect. In this analogy more than any of the others I spy greater unlikeness than likeness.

▪ To begin with, games are for most people forms of recreation. They are diversions—good for a little entertainment now and then. But discipleship to Christ is a matter of life and death (in baptism, the believer dies to sin and the self, 1 Pet 2:24). The gospel is not "just for fun" and worship is no mere pastime.

▪ Second, the ease with which someone might switch between games, abruptly ending one and starting another, is hard to relate to the committed practice of the Christian religion. Christianity cannot simply be picked up and put down at will. It is not meant to be chosen and then dropped as the mood strikes.

■ Third, games, as we have noted, are self-contained systems. But the gospel alleges something different: it is not only for everyone, but about everyone. There are many aspects of the Christian faith that are not self-contained but that make claims on all reality.

■ Fourth, the analogy of games is unavoidably functionalistic. The value of something in a game is its function. What does it do? The same could be said of players—the value of a player in a game is his or her function, and how effectively that function is executed. What does he do and how well does he do it? But the value of the Bible cannot be reduced to its function (as a rule book or a strategy book or whatever). The value of worship cannot be reduced to its effectiveness in attaining a key objective of Christian practice. The value of fellow Christians is not their role in "the game." The result of such thinking is a plague of judgmental attitudes, envy and unhealthy competitiveness. Paul confronts this disease with an analogy from physiology:

> Now the body is not made up of one part but of many. If the foot should say, "Because I am not a hand, I do not belong to the body," it would not for that reason cease to be part of the body. And if the ear should say, "Because I am not an eye, I do not belong to the body," it would not for that reason cease to be part of the body. If the whole body were an eye, where would the sense of hearing be? If the whole body were an ear, where would the sense of smell be? (1 Cor 12:14-17)

Insofar as the analogy of games causes us to value and privilege the things of the faith (including people) according to their usefulness to us, it poses more of a hindrance than a help.

■ The fifth and final weakness of the gaming analogy is the most troublesome. It is difficult—if not impossible—to identify the role of God in the analogy of game. Is God the Father the referee? Is God the Son a hall-of-fame player? Is God the Holy Spirit the coach? Something doesn't feel right about calling the Holy Spirit "coach" or describing the Son as a gifted competitor or visualizing the Father in a black and white striped referee jersey blowing his whistle. The similarities break down beyond repair at this point. There simply are no similarities. It is possible and productive to compare *human* living and doing to the elements of a game, but it does not work well at all to compare *God's* activity in that way. To do that, we will have to wait for a different analogy.

The limitations are not to be neglected, some are quite serious. Nevertheless, as long as we keep them in mind, we can proceed to observe the natural parallels between the structure of games and Christian discipleship.

GOALS: THE END OF THINGS

Christianity is like a game in the sense that it operates according to the four nonsubstitutable ingredients already listed: goals, means, rules and players with right attitudes. Let's begin by considering the goals or ends of Christianity. What objectives are Christians trying to achieve? Many times new converts will say they made a profession of faith because they recognized their sinfulness and need of a redeemer, or more bluntly, because they wanted to be saved, or even more crudely, because they wanted to go to heaven and not hell. The goal of Christian faith for the new convert usually has much to do with the individual's own needs, aspirations and anxieties.

This goal is undeniably self-centered. In a similar way, many kids join team sports initially because they want a trophy. While the thrill of victory is wonderful, eventually players mature and their reasons for playing also mature, such that most committed athletes stick to their sport even when no trophies are offered. Likewise, new believers may naturally have "immature" reasons for committing their lives to Christ, but as they age in the faith, their motives and goals will develop accordingly.

The distinction I am making between mature and immature motives is not intended to patronize or belittle new or young disciples. "Therefore let us stop passing judgment on one another" (Rom 14:13). As our faith grows in maturity, we move away from calculations of rewards and punishments and toward the joy of fellowship with God *for its own sake*, without added incentives. Besides the immediate aims of cleansing sins, being saved and obtaining assurance of eternal life, the larger raison d'être for the Christian faith is found in Christ himself.

Jesus is the final aim and objective. The Scriptures exhort believers to follow Christ (Mt 4:18-22), imitate Christ (1 Cor 11:1), live, work and die, in, through and for Christ (Gal 3:27; Phil 1:21).

Augustine of Hippo (354–430) once declared in a sermon that "the central place they are all coming to is Christ; he is at the center."[4] Maximus the Confessor (580–668), likewise said, "Of all divine mysteries, the mystery of Christ is the most significant, for it teaches us how to situate every present or future perfection of every being, in every kind of intellectual investigation."[5] Christians of all traditions recognize and demand unalloyed and total commitment to Christ.[6] Christ situates our purposes and our pursuits, our goals and our efforts. Christ is at the center of our comings and goings. The thirteenth-century English bishop and saint Richard of Chichester (1197–1253) prayed this memorable prayer:

O most merciful Redeemer, Friend, and Brother,
May I know Thee more clearly,
Love Thee more dearly,
Follow Thee more nearly,
Day by day.[7]

His prayer was converted into lyrics for the 1970s musical *Godspell* and then into a pop rock song by DC Talk on their 1996 multiplatinum album, *Jesus Freak*. Richard of Chichester's "three things" sound out the heartbeat of the Christian walk. They might be called "objectives" or "goals" of the spiritual life, but they function more like vows or prayers. They articulate the most intimate longings of the pilgrim. They represent the maturation of the believer's goals and aims.

Maturity means recognizing the truest and best goals for the Christian life. Second Corinthians declares, "So we make it our goal to please

---

[4]Augustine, Sermon 62A.3, in *Ancient Christian Devotional*, ed. Thomas Oden and Cindy Crosby (Downers Grove, Ill.: InterVarsity Press, 2007), p. 11.
[5]Maximus *Ambigua* line 1332C, quoted in Hans Urs von Balthasar, *Cosmic Liturgy: The Universe According to Maximus the Confessor* (San Francisco: Ignatius, 2003), pp. 208-9.
[6]See Robert Barron, *The Priority of Christ* (Grand Rapids: Brazos, 2007).
[7]See Hugh Lawrence, "St. Richard of Chichester," *Studies in Sussex Church History* (London: Leopard's Head Press, 1981), pp. 35-55.

him, whether we are at home in the body or away from it" (2 Cor 5:9).
In Isaiah the holy and sovereign Lord declares,

> Turn to me and be saved,
>> all you ends of the earth;
>> for I am God, and there is no other.
> By myself I have sworn,
>> my mouth has uttered in all integrity
>> a word that will not be revoked:
> Before me every knee will bow;
>> by me every tongue will swear. (Is 45:22-23)

This irrevocable word is consummated in the person of Christ Jesus.[8]
According to Philippians,

> at the name of Jesus every knee should bow,
>> in heaven and on earth and under the earth,
>> and every tongue confess that Jesus Christ is Lord,
>> to the glory of God the Father. (Phil 2:10-11)

The celebrated first question of the Westminster Shorter Catechism
asks, "What is the chief end of man?" The answer: "To glorify God and
enjoy Him for ever." Praising and honoring the triune God revealed in
Jesus emerges in Scripture and Christian tradition as the true purpose
and destiny of the word and all its inhabitants (Rev 21:1-5).

The chief end of humankind is not only to glorify God but also "*enjoy* Him for ever." Games not only achieve objectives; they are to be
enjoyed. Enjoyment is not just the byproduct of winning the game;
games are inherently pleasurable. Likewise, the practice of Christianity
brings about joy and abundant life—life experienced "to the fullest" (Jn
10:10)—life with God. Augustine exuberantly declares, "The things
which are to be enjoyed, then, are the Father and the Son and the Holy
Spirit, and the Trinity that consists of them, which is a kind of single,
supreme thing, shared by all who enjoy it." Pausing to catch his breathe
and check his enthusiasm, Augustine backtracks at this point, "if indeed it is a thing and not the cause of all things, and if indeed it is a

---

[8]"Creation has an end, creation is to be consummated, and the name of that end and consummation is Jesus" (Stanley Hauerwas, *Cross-Shattered Christ* [Grand Rapids: Brazos, 2004], p. 87).

cause. It is not easy to find a suitable name for such excellence."[9] True enough; the excellence of God does not lend itself to naming. Augustine is right to remind us that God is not simply "a thing" or even "the thing" of our enjoyment; rather we should say Christian discipleship joins God's purposes with our joy, that our joy may be complete (1 Jn 1:4). We were made in God's image to know and be known by our Creator—our deepest desire is also our divinely appointed end.[10] To know Christ and glorify God is to know our created purpose and our greatest pleasure. To our surprise and delight, God's ends match our greatest desires, "since we are God's offspring" (Acts 17:29), and they bring joy and fulfillment that do not dissipate in an afternoon's time.

[9]Augustine *On Christian Teaching* 1.5, translated by R. P. H. Green (New York: Oxford University Press, 1997), p. 10.

[10]John Milbank, *Being Reconciled* (New York: Routledge, 2003), p. 203.

CHRISTIANITY AS GAME

PLAYERS

THE END OF FAITH IS FOUND in the face of Christ—to "see face to face" and to "know fully, even as I am fully known" (1 Cor 13:12). Christianity is like a game in the sense that it has an end, an objective. It is also like a game in the sense that it requires *participants*, people committed to playing the game.

PLAYERS AND TEAMS

Games don't play themselves, people do. Games are made great not because of rules or means or goals, but because of players. Christianity has been graced with some great players, men like Martin Luther King Jr., William Carey and Polycarp, and women like Dorothy Day, Susanna Wesley and Vibia Perpetua. Most of us look to the everyday saints we know—grandmothers, Sunday school teachers, pastors and the like—in order to learn the ropes of Christianity. People do not normally study the rules and regulations in order to learn how to play a game, they look to what other players are doing. So it is in the church.

This can place pressure on public figures, and for this reason James, leader of the Jerusalem church and half-brother of Jesus, warned, "Not many of you should presume to be teachers, my brothers, for you know that we who teach will be judged more strictly" (Jas 3:1). The pressure is a natural one, the same as put on great athletes and sports professionals. It is how we learn to play the game ourselves: by watching, scrutinizing and mimicking our heroes. When those heroes fall, in sports or in church, the pain of betrayal and disappointment is acute. But when the relationship works, it can be inspiring and marvelous.

Even so, caution needs to be thrown up. Christians should be wary of mentor-mentee, master-apprentice arrangements. This might come as a surprising and counterintuitive claim at first. But the mentoring model is unavoidably Greek, as found in Homer's *Odyssey*. King Odysseus assigned Mentor to watch over and educate his son Telemachus while he went away for war. Mentoring relationships formed the basis of the Greek aristocratic society where older men would introduce younger ones to circles of privilege and rank. The model of mentoring operates on the ground of unequal power, special selection and exclusion. At its base level, it promotes discrimination, secrecy, favoritism and subordination.

By contrast, Christian fellowship is one of equals, of "brothers and sisters" and "holy partners in a heavenly calling" (Heb 3:1 NRSV). There should be no "favoritism" (Jas 2:1). We are all fellow travelers on the road to God (Heb 11:13-16). Acts 2:44 describes the early church as a place in which "all the believers were together and had everything in common." This is a model to strive for. Galatians 3 makes clear that in the church "there is neither Jew nor Greek, slave nor free, male nor female; for you are all one in Christ Jesus" (Gal 3:28). First Peter insists that the church, taken as a whole, is "a chosen people, a royal priesthood, a holy nation" (1 Pet 2:9).

And yet, there is a real tension, even in the New Testament, on this point. The New Testament church is founded upon radical equality in Christ, but it is organized around leadership and order. Natural and proper distinctions within the body of Christ can arise for many reasons. Who would deny that the aged Simeon and the prophetess Anna, because of their hard-earned and time-tested maturity in the faith, were granted the privilege above many others to recognize the infant Christ-child in the temple (Lk 2:25-28)? The more experienced and mature among us must be respected, listened to and consulted. In addition to the natural delineation between the beginner and the well-practiced, there are other biblical distinctions within the church. In

Ephesians we are told that our Lord "gave some to be apostles, some to be prophets, some to be evangelists, and some to be pastors and teachers" (Eph 4:11). Just as one tribe out of Israel's twelve was divinely chosen to supply priests and attend to the worship and sacrifices on behalf of all the people, so a handful of people in the church are called, appointed and specially ordained to different ministries. The New Testament recognizes the need for various offices: bishops ("overseers"), deacons ("servants"), apostles ("messengers"), etc. (1 Tim 3).

It should nevertheless be kept in mind that the rationale for these agencies is never power or prestige, but, as Ephesians explains:

> It was he who gave some to be apostles, some to be prophets, some to be evangelists, and some to be pastors and teachers, to prepare God's people for works of service, so that the body of Christ may be built up until we all reach unity in the faith and in the knowledge of the Son of God and become mature, attaining to the whole measure of the fullness of Christ. (Eph 4:11-13)

Some are called out and specially tasked not for the sake of division or hierarchy, but so that the body of Christ as a whole be built up and better united.[1] And, especially relevant here, so that we all attain to *maturity* in the faith.

For disciples, there is only one High Priest (Heb 7–8) and Master (Mt 23:10): the Lord and King Jesus Christ. And even Jesus dispenses with the title of Master, saying, "I no longer call you servants, because a servant does not know his master's business. Instead I have called you friends" (Jn 15:15). Instead of mentor-mentee, master-apprentice configurations, Christian discipleship and training should take the form of "subversive friendships"—radically real, honest and equal.

One of the very first teaching manuals circulated among churches was the *Didache* ("The 'Teaching' of the Twelve Apostles"). Its text was lost to the world for years and years until it serendipitously resurfaced in a monastic library in Constantinople in 1873. The *Didache* contains instructions on matters of worship, church polity and behavior. Schol-

---

[1]The same principle of unity should be applied to the various "household rules" given in Eph 5:22–6:9; Col 3:18–4:1 and Tit 2:1-10.

ars are uncertain of its date of composition and its authorship, but it seems to have been produced within the first one hundred years of Christianity's existence. It offers a window into the thinking and day-to-day practices of the earliest believers.[2]

Calling for respectful treatment of youth, children, slaves and servants, both male and female, the *Didache* says, "he [Christ] does not come to call those of high status, but those whom the Spirit has prepared."[3] This ancient church manual also encourages congregations to be hospitable to teachers and prophets who might pass through their doors or arise from within, but not uncritically or slavishly. A teacher should be approved and given an audience only "if his teaching brings righteousness and the knowledge of the Lord" and only if he does not "teach something different," or "ask for money," or stay more than two days.[4] Believers are admonished to "exercise your critical judgment," and then "you will know him."[5]

There is no automatic hierarchy or power-position within the body of Christ because all serve the same Lord and are held to the same standard. Therefore, every member of the church has a responsibility to "reprimand one another," not in anger, "but in peace, as you have learned from the gospel."[6] The *Didache* wisely recognizes that the primary causes of disruption to pure worship are power struggles and stubborn hostilities. "Let no one quarreling with his neighbor join you until they are reconciled, that your sacrifice many not be defiled."[7]

We learn how to play not by playing alone but by playing with other people. So also the Christian faith must be practiced with other committed Christians in communal worship, not merely in private moments of prayer. "Gather together frequently," says the *Didache*, "seeking what is appropriate for your souls."[8] Christians exercise their faith in group

---

[2]Also see Tony Jones, *The Teaching of the Twelve: Believing and Practicing the Primitive Christianity of the Ancient Didache Community* (Brewster, Mass.: Paraclete Press, 2009).
[3]*Didache*, 4:10, in *The Apostolic Fathers*, vol. 1, trans. Bart Ehrman (Cambridge, Mass.: Harvard University Press, 2003).
[4]Ibid., 11:1-12.
[5]Ibid., 12:1.
[6]Ibid., 15:3.
[7]Ibid., 14:2.
[8]Ibid., 16:2.

activities like singing, proclaiming, collecting tithes and offerings, and studying the Bible together. This is a group game. Undoubtedly, benefit can be derived from studying Scripture on one's own, praying in silence and so forth, just as shooting hoops alone can improve skills. Even so, shooting baskets alone only makes all the more obvious the group nature of the game of basketball. Having "quiet times" with God serves to highlight our need for accountability, collective worship and fellowship.[9]

The other side of the coin is this: Groups (whether small or large) only function well together when there is order, organization and leadership. Group games operate most effectively when there are team-captains, coaches, officials, time-keepers, referees, and so on. So also Christian community was from the earliest days organized around overseers, elders, deacons and other ministers. By the sixth chapter of Acts, the burgeoning Jerusalem community of believers found itself in need of organization and division of labor, and so selected seven men for the daily distribution of food (Acts 6:1-6). In the same era as the anonymous *Didache*, Ignatius (d. 107), the Syrian bishop of Antioch, was arrested on account of his Christian witness and sent to Rome to suffer execution. In transit, he dashed off several short letters to various churches, including those in Ephesus, Smyrna, Philadelphia, Tralles and Magnesia, reminding, admonishing and pleading them to stay true to their bishop, that is, to the head minister who oversaw their regions. The greatly revered Ignatius exhorted the churches to "submit" to the bishop and be "united with your bishop" and "do nothing without the bishop."[10]

The apparent patriarchal authoritarianism of Ignatius's epistles might strike readers as contrary to the more communal and egalitarian spirit of the *Didache*. We might be tempted to think these two testimonies represented two different strands of early Christianity. This con-

---

[9]Tim Conder questions the very notion of something like a "personal faith," suggesting that the term may in fact be a misnomer (Tim Conder, *The Church in Transition: The Journey of Existing Churches into the Emerging Culture* [Grand Rapids: Zondervan, 2006], pp. 47-49).

[10]Ignatius of Antioch, "To the Magnesians," sect. 6-7; "To the Philadelphians," sect. 7-8; "To the Smyrnaeans," sect. 9, *Ancient Christian Writers*, vol. 1, trans. James Kleist (New York: Paulist Press, 1946), pp. 70-71, 87-88, 93.

clusion would be incorrect. In every letter, Ignatius articulates the greater goal at stake: *unity*. Submission to the bishop, respect for church authority and the resolution of petty quarrels all have one aim: "to strive to do all things in harmony with God."[11] "Let there be nothing among you tending to divide you," but in all things be united.[12] In this sense, Ignatius's goal is the same as the *Didache*'s. The *Didache* also shares a commitment to unity, as is evident from its advice, "Do not create a schism, but bring peace to those who are at odds" and from its prayer, "may your church be gathered together from the ends of the earth into your kingdom."[13] Although their style and needs may be different, both the bishop Ignatius and the *Didache* recognize the same greater purpose. Order, offices, discipline and command all serve a greater good—the unity of the fellowship.

The game of Christianity requires players who play well with one another. The community of the saints requires the unity of the saints. The purpose of organized unity is not more committee work, more unassailable bureaucracies, or more control over individuals, but the glory of God, the testimony to truth, the service of the world and the welcoming of others into the game.

SPORTING ATTITUDE

Turning our attention from the makeup of the team of players, we need to consider the "attitude" of the players. Games require participants with *right attitudes*, that is, sporting intentions. Players are expected to follow the rules and play fairly. They are also expected to give it their best effort and play the best they can. If a player cheats or plays half-heartedly, the game fails. These expectations do not usually come in the form of written rules, they are unspoken. They represent the "spirit" of the game.

---

[11]Ignatius "To the Magnesians" 6, p. 70. Another contemporary of Ignatius and the *Didache*, Clement, offers similar admonishments to unity, comparing the church to an army, with a chain of command from generals down to foot-soldiers. Clement of Rome, "First Epistle to the Corinthians," sect. 37, *Ancient Christian Writers*, vol. 1, p. 32.

[12]Ignatius "To the Magnesians" 6, p. 71.

[13]*Didache* 9:4. Not only does the *Didache* share a commitment to unity with Ignatius, it also shares respect for bishops and deacons, as well as prophets (*Didache* 15:1-2).

Christianity must also be enacted and practiced in a certain "spirit." St. Cyril of Jerusalem (c. 315–386) led catechetical classes at his church for new Christians in the middle part of the fourth century. The classes ran for forty days, after which the initiates would be baptized and become members of the church. During the very first session, Cyril would say, "Perhaps you have come with a different motive: perhaps you are courting, and a girl is your reason—or, conversely, a boy. Many a time, too, a slave has wished to please his master, or a friend his friend."[14] Not everyone who enters and joins the church does it for the right reasons. Some are just trying to get a date. Cyril's word on this is: "It is of no use your body being here if your thoughts and heart are elsewhere."[15] The convert is expected to commit "with all of your soul and with all your strength and with all your mind" to the Lord and Savior, Jesus Christ (Lk 10:27). No one should enter lightly into covenant with Christ. Jesus recommends that potential recruits "count the costs" before deciding to follow, as would any good architect before starting to build or military general before leading the charge, because "any of you who does not give up everything he has cannot be my disciple" (Lk 14:33). In response to the would-be follower who first asks permission to return home and say farewell to his family before throwing in his lot with the wandering rabbi, Jesus says, "No one who puts his hand to the plow and looks back is fit for the kingdom of God" (Lk 9:62). That is to say, practicing the Christian faith requires that one commit to it with one's entire life. "God requires of us only one thing, sincerity."[16]

Is the "game" comparison appropriate here? Do "right attitude" and "sporting intention" capture what is at stake? Here again we bump up against the limit of our analogy. Talking about the "sporting attitude" of Christian disciples possibly stretches the game analogy beyond what it can

---

[14]Cyril of Jerusalem *Procatechesis* 5, trans. Leo McCauley and Anthony Stephenson, The Fathers of the Church, vol. 61 (Washington, D.C.: Catholic University of America Press, 1968), p. 74.

[15]Ibid., 2, p. 70.

[16]Ibid., 8, p. 77. "You have entered for a race: run the course; you will not get the like chance again. If it were your wedding day that was fixed, would you not, ignoring everything else, be wholly engaged in preparations for the marriage feast? Then, on the eve of consecrating your soul to your heavenly Spouse, will you not put by the things of the body to win those of the spirit?" (Cyril of Jerusalem *Procatechesis* 6, pp. 75-76).

bear. "Attitude" language tends to reduce things to the level of pop psychology, hardly fit for a junior high lesson. There is more at stake than sportsmanship. The mature disciple of Christ is more than a good sport.

We might be able to salvage the analogy by remembering that just as any game is best played when played fairly and competitively, so Christianity is best practiced without reservations and with one's whole self. There is a certain *spirit* or intentionality expected of the believer's attitude (e.g., Ps 51:10; Is 26:9).

St. Francis of Assisi (1182–1226) exemplified better than anyone in his age the proper "sporting" attitude—the true spirit of Christian commitment. He performed his Christian duties with a skill and dexterity matched by few others. He provides us with a model to imitate. Perhaps best remembered as the patron saint of animals and the environment (you will often find his statue in gardens because he preached humility to the birds, tranquility to the wolves and even trees were said to bend to his words). Francis devoted his life—body, soul, material possessions and all—to Christ. He joked that when he adopted God as his father, he took Lady Poverty as his wife. He gave up all worldly goods and renounced his family name and privilege in order to dwell among the poor and sick and rejected.

His renunciation of material niceties did not spring from morbid self-hatred or hatred of the world, but from a simple obedience of the teachings of Jesus. He never wavered in his intention to follow Christ; he never attempted to "cheat" the system or find ways around his calling. When Jesus, that Man of Sorrows who had no place to lay his head, said to sell everything and follow him, Francis took him at his word. He did just that. Francis was serenely confident that Christ "will not deprive us of our bodily necessities when we need them."[17] His

---

[17]Donald Spoto, *Reluctant Saint: The Life of Francis of Assisi* (New York: Penguin Compass, 2002), p. 92. St. Antony of Egypt likewise refused material possessions, and also considered his actions neither courageous nor heroic. For him, it was an act of simple obedience. As he explains in his own words:

> No one, once he has rejected the world, should think that he has left behind anything of importance, because the whole earth, compared to the infinity of the heavens, is small and limited. Even if we renounce the whole world, we cannot give anything in exchange which is of similar value to the heavenly dwellings. If each person considers this he will immediately realize that if he abandons a few acres of land or a small house or a moderate

simple trust in Jesus won the hearts of many. Young men and women began to seek him out and commit themselves to his way of life. The group grew into a movement.

"It seems to me that your life is very rough and hard," the local bishop of Assisi once told him, "especially because you do not possess anything." Francis replied with straightforward honesty, "If we had possessions, my lord bishop, we would need arms for our protection—because disputes and lawsuits, as you know, usually arise out of possessions. And so, love of God and neighbor are greatly impeded. Therefore, we do not want to possess anything."[18]

Once a mother of two sons, both of whom had joined Francis's company, came to Francis in desperation. She had no money and no food and was destitute. Francis went and asked his comrades if there was anything in the community of value that could be given to her. Nothing was found, as Francis and his followers were committed to poverty. The only thing that they collectively possessed was a copy of the New Testament, for the reading of the lessons. Books being very precious, expensive and hard to come by in the days before the printing press, Francis did not hesitate, but said, "Give her the New Testament so she can sell it for her needs. I firmly believe that the Lord and *his* mother will be pleased more by giving it to her than if we read from it."[19] The mother accepted the book and sold it in return for enough money to live for two years. Francis said it would be better for the altar and its adornments stripped and the love of Christ kept than to have the altar decorated and the way of Christ despised.[20]

Now, Francis did not expect everyone to do as he did and give up their possessions. He did not preach guilt, only the simple message of the gospel: "Love and fear God, and reform your lives."[21] "Give to others, and it shall be given to you. Forgive and you shall be forgiven. And

---

sum of gold, he ought not to feel proud of himself in the belief that he has given up a lot. (Athanasius *Life of St. Antony* 17, in *Early Christian Lives*, ed. Carolinne White [New York: Penguin, 1998], p. 20)

[18]Spoto, *Reluctant Saint*, p. 76.
[19]Ibid., pp. 174-75.
[20]Ibid.
[21]Ibid., p. 78.

if you do not forgive others their sins, the Lord will not forgive you your sins."[22] Francis did not cajole but inspired people to good works.

It may seem to some readers that I am idealizing the example of Francis. But of course, he was not perfect. Besides Jesus of Nazareth, there is no perfect example of human saintliness; imperfections, miscalculations and conflict must also be attended to as we search for the spirit of Christian behavior. Sometimes the enthusiasm of Francis's followers swelled into an unhealthy extremism whereby they would punish their bodies for "intemperance," "wantonness" or elevated body temperature brought on by impure thoughts. Thomas of Celano, the first biographer of Francis, records that "they were so single-minded in their efforts to quell the urges of the flesh by mortification that they would often actually strip naked in the iciest weather and plunge thorns into themselves all over their bodies until they were covered in blood."[23] Francis himself occasionally gave in to bouts of extremism. His biographer admiringly reports that once after Francis had indulged in a "small portion of chicken" he had been craving, he was overwhelmed by the guilt of his gluttony.

> He went to Assisi, and when he came to the city gate he told the Brother who was with him to tie a rope around his neck and drag him through the streets all round the city like a robber, and to shout at the top of his voice: "Here! Come and see this glutton who has been stuffing himself with poultry behind your backs!" Of course, people flocked to see this extraordinary sight, but then they sighed and sighed again, and said as they wept together: "What hope is there for us, whose whole lives are spent in bloodshed, who nourish our souls and bodies on immorality and drunkenness?" So their consciences were pricked, and Francis' shining example challenged them to lead better lives.[24]

Although Thomas the biographer is awe-inspired by the degree of Francis's self-mortification, it seems clear that St. Francis's penitentiary

---

[22]Ibid., p. 98.

[23]Thomas of Celano, *The First Life of Saint Francis of Assisi* (London: SPCK, 2000), §40, p. 44. It is not clear that Francis approved of these measures; indeed Aidan House shows that he disallowed them once he became aware of the practices (*Francis of Assisi* [Mahwah, N.J.: Hidden Spring, 2001], p. 152).

[24]Celano, *Saint Francis*, §52, p. 54.

self-abuse over minor pleasures and indulgences represents not the perfection of devotion but its fermentation. Spiritual discernment must be exercised. Some stories about Francis spur the believer on to greater action and others illustrate enthusiasm gone awry. Just as enthusiasm for a sport can sometimes turn into unhealthy mania, especially among over-zealous fans, so passion for the gospel can become distorted and disfigured by megalomania, self-hatred, obsession, prejudice and fear.

The opposite extreme, whereby enthusiasm and devotion is constricted and even snuffed out by law and order, can also pose a threat. Francis preferred spontaneity and disliked the idea of organizing, training and managing the growing number of followers and adherents. Bureaucracy involves compromise. Nevertheless, because of the group's growing size and because of the desire to preach in other venues besides Assisi, Francis trekked to Rome in 1209 to ask for the pope's blessing on his and his companions' way of life. Pope Innocent III reluctantly granted approval to the group, but with a condition: they would have to give up some of their cherished freedom and submit to papal control. He personally tonsured Francis and his brothers, making them clerics. In so doing, Innocent III put them directly under church authority.

Eventually, Franciscan freedom was further constrained when the pope appointed Cardinal Ugolino (who was subsequently elected Pope Gregory IX) to oversee and regulate the group—this while Francis was still alive and supposedly in charge. Ugolino began to give shape, authority and his own purpose to the movement. Disgusted with the tightening of the structure, Francis resigned his position of Minister General and withdrew from his namesake order. "From now on, I am dead to you."[25]

With Francis first sidelined and then shortly thereafter deceased, the rules of poverty were gradually loosened and service to Rome was increased. For a time the Franciscan movement was in serious danger of being reduced to nothing more than a political tool or even weapon of popes Innocent and Gregory. The pope's "sporting attitude" could be judged deficient because he manipulated the Franciscan order for his

---

[25]Spoto, *Reluctant Saint*, p. 173.

own ends. Analogously, a team coach might be judged unsportsman-like for trying to unduly influence his players' performance for some ulterior motive.

There needs to be a balance with regards to dedication or what we have been calling "the spirit of the game." The right spirit can be located on a continuum or a scale in between excess and deficiency. Francis's desire for purity and Christ-like holiness was good in itself, but at times it tilted towards an extreme of self-hatred and self-abuse. The church authorities' desire for order and organization in the Franciscan move-ment was likewise good in itself, but at times it gave way to spirit-killing authoritarianism. At one end of the "spirit" or "attitude" continuum we judge the actions of the church authorities deficient because they were manipulative; at the other end we judge some of the actions of Francis and his followers to be excessive because they caused bodily harm.

The Christian spirit lies somewhere between these two extremes in something like Aristotle's Golden Mean. In his *Nicomachean Ethics*, the world's first textbook on the subject of ethics, Aristotle (384–322 B.C.) says that virtue "aims at hitting the mean" between the extremes of "excess" and "deficiency."[26] Aristotle offers some wonderfully useful examples to explain his meaning: a healthy eater neither overconsumes nor undereats; a physically fit athlete neither overexerts nor under-trains; a disciplined money-manager neither hordes nor fritters his gain; a courageous soldier neither rushes foolhardy into danger nor shrinks from it in cowardice.

> It is a mean between two kinds of vice, one of excess and the other of deficiency; and also for this reason, that whereas these vices fall short of or exceed the right measure in both feelings and actions, virtue discov-ers the mean and chooses it. Thus from the point of view of its essence and the definition of its real nature, virtue is a mean; but in respect of what is right and best, it is an extreme.[27]

Virtue is not simply the least offensive or most neutral of choices, it represents the *best* choice. The Greek word for "virtue" that Aristotle

---

[26]Aristotle *The Nicomachean Ethics* 2.6, trans. J. A. K. Thomson (New York: Penguin Books, 2004), p. 41.
[27]Ibid., p. 42.

employs here is *arête*, which can also be translated "excellence." The spirit of Christian action is its own form of excellence, and it is a balance between extremes and deficiencies.

Nevertheless, we may still want to ask: how does one know if excellence has been achieved? How can one be sure that his or her attitudes, intentions and actions are right before God? Aristotle thought the Golden Mean could be easily "determined by a rational principle, and by that which a prudent man would use to determine it."[28] Any prudent person should be able to strike a balance between the extremes. However, in practice this does not always happen; it did not happen every time for Francis or the church authorities of his day. Why should it for us? The human brain has an amazing ability to justify itself and its attitudes, be they right or wrong.

In order to play the game properly, we still need to investigate the tools and rules of Christianity. Attitudes and actions are best kept in check by rules and by the right use of the equipment we have been given. We will next turn attention to the equipment, or tools, of the faith, and then to their rules of use.

---

[28]Ibid.

11

CHRISTIANITY AS GAME

EQUIPMENT

EQUIPMENT, INSTRUMENTS AND GEAR can include any number of things: from a board and dice to a stopwatch and a track. In soccer, having a ball is a key ingredient, but it alone is not enough. One must also find a field or at least a level playing area and two clearly marked goals. Some of these elements might be improvised and approximated, as in street ball—but equipment is never optional, it is essential. The means for practicing Christianity are what theologians typically call the "sources" or "sources of authority." However, "sources of authority" tends to connote something static, sterile and stringent. We are not talking so much about the *authority* for believing this or that much as the *resources* for spiritual formation—the equipment for Christian life.

By "equipment," "means" or "resources" I want to include a lot of things: Scripture, history and tradition, the community of faith, teachers and ministers, the personal experience of the believer, and the movement of God's Spirit. But immediately there is something terribly wrong with the language of "resources," "equipment," "tools" and "means." It is unavoidably functionalistic and individualistic. "Resources" are things I as an individual use or dispense with as they suit my needs. They can be picked up, put down and replaced. They are external to the self. They are objects at the user's disposal. They have significance and value in relation to the user only and not in themselves. The user determines their worth. But surely the Bible, the tradition, the community and the rest are not *just* resources. Their value is not limited to their usefulness to the individual. Nor are they simply "tools" or "equipment" for the Christian life. To call them such is to reduce their value and meaning to their function. So, for instance, it is not the case that the Bible is holy and authoritative only insofar as an individual sees it that way or uses it that way.

Again we see a way that Christianity is both like but also unlike a game. The functionalist and individualistic danger might be avoided and the game analogy might be kept if we consider that the items required for playing any game are themselves *part of the game*. They are integral to the game itself and cannot be transferred or substituted without seriously jeopardizing the game. In a game of Rook the cards are essential. It would be unfair to play with either a partial deck or an overloaded one. Likewise, it would be ridiculous to swap Rook cards for Go Fish cards, still expecting to play Rook. The right number and kind of cards are a prerequisite without which the game will not work, or at least not work properly and fairly. In the same way, when I list off the elements involved in the practice of Christianity, I mean to specify those items without which Christianity cannot operate. These are *essential* ingredients in the sense that they pertain to the essence of practicing the faith. Here is a brief checklist of essential equipment:

The Bible. The Bible is probably the first essential element or resource of the faith that comes to mind. This is "The Book," God's holy Word to humanity. Not only does it witness to God's revelation, it *is* God's revelation, wrapped in human words and stories and preserved by the Christian tradition. The God who is Father, Son and Spirit is made known in the pages of the Bible as the Spirit of Christ encounters readers personally and as the community of faith guides those same readers in understanding what they read. The Bible is so central to the practice of Christianity that without it nothing Christians do will make much sense. It is at the heart of the game. More will be said about the Bible in the next chapter.

Lived convictions. By "lived convictions," I mean to suggest the totality of one's pilgrimage with God, all of the beliefs and practices which have been cobbled together over time to make the disciple of

Christ. I can tell the story of my lived convictions—how I was raised in a Christian home, what my earliest ideas and struggles were, when I "accepted" Jesus as my Lord and Savior, was baptized, felt a call to ministry, enrolled in seminary and so on. It is a story of my experience with God, the faith and the church.

I use the expression "lived convictions" as opposed to talking about my "experiences" with God because "experience" comes across as individualistic and secretive—my "experience" is my own private possession, it cannot be challenged. Indeed, "religious experience" is regularly conceived as a personal moment of spiritual ecstasy or enlightenment during worship or prayer. Too often we reduce our journey of faith to a single instant in time—"When were you saved?" All that matters is that at some point in your life you prayed the prayer of salvation and had a saving "experience." Religious experience becomes something singular, exceptional and instantaneous.

By contrast, I want to suggest that the whole of our being and history must be taken into account, viewed through the gospel, informed by the Spirit and put in the context of the fellowship of believers. This is a life journey; the Christian faith demands heart, mind and body; these are lived convictions.[1]

Convictions are the game pieces through which we live those beliefs and commitments held nearest and dearest to our souls. "I believe in God" is a conviction that constitutes a central feature of my personal identity. Convictions call out who we really are—who I really am. Convictions are so persistent and so deep-rooted that changing them

---

[1] The U.S. court systems are very hesitant to define "religion," "belief" or "religious belief," and routinely strike down laws that do. For instance, in 1996 the courts struck down a Massachusetts law because its application was limited to "established religions" and so was not broad enough to account for unestablished or unrecognized religious practices. *Pielech v. Massasoit Greyhound, Inc.*, 668 N.E.2d 1298 (Mass. 1996). In the United Kingdom, where the court systems are not as constricted by a strong separation of church-state doctrine, the courts have issued helpful and instructive definitions: "Belief means more than just 'mere opinions or deeply held feelings'; there must be a holding of spiritual or philosophical convictions which have an identifiable formal content." *McFeekly v UK: (1981), 3 EHRR 161.* "The term 'beliefs' . . . denotes a certain level of cogency, seriousness, cohesion, and importance." *Campbell and Cosans v. UK: (1982), 4 EHRR 293 para 36.* These definitions help draw out three items of critical importance: beliefs must have form and content; they must be more than opinion and feeling; they must result in action.

changes one's identity.[2] I might stop believing in God, but to do so, to really do so, would mean much more than the change of one little idea. It would change everything about me: my attitudes about the Bible, the meaning of life, prayer, attending church, giving money, etc. Convictions are deeply held beliefs that express our faith, hope and love.

Lived convictions clothe, guard and defend us like armor. Ephesians tells us to put on the full armor of God, the uniform and protective padding of the game.

> Stand firm then, with the belt of truth buckled around your waist, with the breastplate of righteousness in place, and with your feet fitted with the readiness that comes from the gospel of peace. In addition to all this, take up the shield of faith, with which you can extinguish all the flaming arrows of the evil one. Take the helmet of salvation and the sword of the Spirit, which is the word of God. (Eph 6:14-17)

The bronze helmet of salvation, the shield of faith, the winged shoes of peace and the shimmering righteousness that we strap across our chest: these are convictions we wear. Faith, righteousness, salvation, truth, peace—these are more than abstract ideas; they constitute the armor of God, the uniform of the soldier of Christ, the proper attire for the game.

Proper attire is necessary for participating in most games, and that is especially true for practicing Christianity. The lived convictions of faith, salvation, peace and righteousness are a must. This is not simply an academic project or a matter of intellectual curiosity, it demands personal involvement, commitment and witness. Playing the game well involves full participation. Christianity must be lived.

Community. Christianity is a team sport. Community is not an option for the believer. To become a Christian is to discover you have been made a newborn in a new family, it is to become a member of a larger body, a citizen of a different country, a living stone finding its place in the building. The church is a breast of nourishment to the newborn, a garden of good fruit, vegetables and plentiful shade, a true path that

---

[2]James McClendon and James Smith, *Convictions: Diffusing Religious Relativism*, rev. ed. (Valley Forge, Penn.: Trinity Press International, 1994), p. 5.

"circumscribes the whole world," and a bulwark against "the misfortunes that meet the race of men by necessity."[3] John Zizioulas is right to say, "The Church is not simply an institution. She is a 'mode of existence,' *a way of being*."[4] The church (as in the church universal) includes local churches, small group fellowships and families as well as the wider fellowships of believers found in associations, denominations and so on. These are all expressions of the one body. Despite all appearances to the contrary, Christianity is not a federation of independent churches and denominations. Christianity consists of the one people of God and one communion of faith that speaks many tongues in many lands.

Tradition. Most of our forms of worship, our hymns and songs, our church administration, our core beliefs, our ethics and even our architecture has been handed down to us by brothers and sisters in the faith who came before us. What we have is not of our own invention.[5] All of this can be called "tradition," a word which comes from the Latin meaning "what is handed down." In this sense, the tradition not only includes the important theologians, councils, commentaries and creeds of the past, it embraces the liturgy, worship styles, pews and pulpits.

Tradition is what shapes the lived convictions of communities. Tradition helps us to think through the gospel, find our place in the great Christian heritage and be formed by the faith. It continually works to situate our worship, prayer, experience and Bible reading within the wider community of the faithful down through the ages.

The leadership of the Spirit. The Holy Spirit is the empowering presence of God in the world, the Scriptures and the church. The game does not progress without the direction and leadership of God's Spirit. Jesus told his disciples on the last night of his earthly life, "But the Counselor, the Holy Spirit, whom the Father will send in my name, will teach you all things, and remind you of everything I have said to you" (Jn 14:26). The Spirit guides us into all truth (Jn 16:13).

---

[3]Irenaeus *Against Heresies* 5.20, ANF, vol. 1, p. 549; Origen *On Prayer* 5.3, *Origen*, Classics of Western Spirituality, ed. by Rowan Green (New York: Paulist Press, 1998), p. 91.

[4]John Zizioulas, *Being as Communion* (Crestwood, N.Y.: St. Vladimir's Seminary Press, 1997), p. 15.

[5]Jaroslav Pelikan, *The Christian Tradition*, vol. 1: *The Emergence of the Catholic Tradition* (Chicago: University of Chicago Press, 1971), p. 9.

A word of caution: here the game analogy breaks down and becomes almost inoperable. The leadership and assurance of the Spirit cannot be treated as a piece of equipment or a tool. Gaming implements are impersonal objects. The Spirit is God's personal presence (Ps 139:7). We might be tempted to give the comparison a more personal dimension by comparing the work of the Holy Spirit with the work of a coach, but that is not quite right either. God's Holy Spirit does not stand on the sidelines, barking out plays and calling time-outs. The image of the coach is too external and too simplistic.

The holy presence of God inspires, forgives, enlivens, makes new, encourages, energizes, teaches, equips, heals and resurrects. God is not far removed from human activity, but present in Spirit, *Immanuel*, God with us as a "sanctifying power, in which all are said to have a share who have deserved to be sanctified by His grace."[6] So testifies Origen. His intellectual predecessor at Alexandria, Clement (150–c. 215), agrees, "In His own Spirit He says He will deck the body of the Word; as certainly by his own Spirit He will nourish those who hunger for the Word."[7] Against all expectations, the Creator enters creation, the Word enters words, the Spirit bedecks the body and reaches to the center of human experience in order to participate in human history from the inside out. Of course, God's participation is always transformative; when the Spirit shares in our world, our world is upended and overturned. God's Spirit makes the game real.

These five elements—the Bible, lived convictions, community, tradition and the leadership of the Spirit—are the bare bones of Christianity. They are essential to living faithfully, worshiping truthfully and witnessing boldly. Beware of the next question that comes to mind: Which of these is most important? Which comes first? I want to argue that although this is indeed a natural question, it is not the right one to ask. It is a false move because equipment cannot be ordered or given hierarchy: equipment works in relation.

---

[6]Origen *De Principiis* 1.1.3, ANF, vol. 4, p. 242. The work of sanctification, in which the Spirit "reveals spiritual knowledge," is the work of training, teaching, preparing and practicing. The contest of faith is best performed under the constant tutelage, encouragement, and instruction of the Spirit.

[7]Clement of Alexandria *The Instructor* 1.6, ANF, vol. 2, p. 221.

Items of equipment might be singled out for the sake of discussion, but in reality they are intimately linked. They come as a package deal. These five elements are more like a web of practices than a list of ideas. That is to say, if one element is either overlooked or overplayed, the others suffer. If someone wanted to play Monopoly but neglected the money (or neglected everything but the money), the game would not function properly, or at least would not be enjoyable. If someone else wanted to play badminton but did not bring a net or rackets, thinking only the shuttlecock was important, that person would be sorely disappointed.

So, no particular priority is implied by the order of these means, they are all needed. However, some people might object still and claim that the *Bible* must surely be the most important. And yet, without the *Spirit* directing and inspiring David, Habakkuk, Luke, John and the other authors, would there even be a Bible? In a similar way, would we have a Bible without the *tradition*, that is, the early church hammering out which books would be included in the Bible and then faithfully transmitting them down through the ages to us? Without the *community* and its guidance, we would not know how to interpret the Bible in the here and now. Without *lived convictions* regarding God's involvement in our lives and in worship, we would have no reason to relate to the community or its Scripture nor would we be open to its teaching.

How do I know God in Christ? Through the biblical story of Israel, Jesus and the church. Why should I trust the Bible's account of these things? Because I recognize the voice God's Spirit in them. How can I trust my own judgment of such matters? Because it agrees with and has been formed by the community of the faithful and the tradition of the faith from ages past. The line of reasoning sounds circular, but I would contend that it is *webbish*. Each source is delicately linked to each other source in a web that constitutes the Christian heritage. Each strand of the web depends on the others, and if one is compromised, so are the others. Some believers become fixated on their own lived convictions, others on the tradition and others on unlocking the mysteries of the Spirit. The result of imbalance is dysfunction.

Here we might appeal to the principle set forth by Clement of Alexandria, who said with regards to the relation of faith and knowledge, that faith is to knowledge as the Father is to the Son. "Now neither is knowledge without faith, nor faith without knowledge. Nor is the Father without the Son; for the Son is with the Father."[8] By similar application, we can say that the Bible is not without tradition, nor is the community of lived convictions without either of these. And all are held together by the Spirit of God, just as the Father, Son and Spirit are held together by their shared love and purpose and being.[9]

Even as I try to redescribe the relationships between the spoken Word, the written Word, the incarnate Word, the communally embodied Word and the personally lived Word [10] and argue for a holistic and balanced view of the different elements, I recognize that special attention must be given to the Bible. What kind of book is this? What are the rules for handling it? For some, the Bible is a thicket of stories, prophecies and prescriptions. For others, it is a no-nonsense rule book. And for still others, it is an antiquated collection of tales from a lost age. Here, perhaps more than elsewhere, we need help. If we get this part wrong, everything else we say and do will not ring true. Just as in the game of football, the ball holds a special place in relation to the other pieces of equipment, and there are explicit regulations for handling it, so Scripture must be handled with special care and sensitivity.

---

[8]Clement of Alexandria *The Stromata* 5.1, ANF, vol. 2, p. 444.

[9]For the classic account, see Karl Barth, *Church Dogmatics* 1/1 and 1/2: *The Doctrine of the Word of God*, trans. G. W. Bromiley (Edinburgh: T & T Clark, 1975).

[10]Here I borrow language and logic from Karl Barth, *Church Dogmatics* 1/1, pp. 88-124.

CHRISTIANITY AS GAME

READING RULES

IT ALMOST GOES WITHOUT SAYING: before a person plays a game he or she must learn *how* to play. Whether by sitting down and reading the rules, or being told how to play, or simply watching others until you figure it out yourself, learning to play is an essential element that should not be overlooked. No one enjoys reading the rule book, but rules are essential for enjoying the game. Rules and procedures can include everything from the number of players allowed in the game to the amount of time allotted for play. It can include how to handle various objects in play and what counts as a score. In some games, players cannot touch the ball with their hands, only their feet. In others just the opposite is true. In this chapter I want to think about the rules for "using" the Bible and give some broad principles for interpreting the text.

An immediate objection might be: do we really need special rules for reading the Bible? Shouldn't we read it just like any other book? Yes and no. Yes, the Bible *is* a book like other books with words, sentences, plots, characters, etc. In fact, the Bible is a collection of sixty-six books written over the course of hundreds of years by a diverse set of authors living in different places and sometimes using different languages. Within its pages the reader is confronted with a cornucopia of literary material—poetry, history, prophecy, philosophy and personal correspondence. Even at the surface level, then, the Bible will challenge the accomplished reader. But we must also respond to the objection by saying: no, the Bible is not like other books, nor should it be read that way. The Bible claims to be something more than a book, more than a collection of stories or facts. It bears witness to divine revelation (Is 1:2; Jer 10:1-2; Eze 1:3; Hos 1:1-2; Obad 1:1) and to divine action in human history (God's calling of Abram out of Ur; the salvation of the Israelites from slavery; the virgin birth of Jesus; the outpouring of the Spirit on the disciples). We encounter this God revealed in the pages of Scripture, as Dietrich Bonhoeffer (1906–1945) says,

> We become a part of what once took place for our salvation. Forgetting and losing ourselves, we, too, pass through the Red Sea, through the desert, across the Jordan into the promised land. With Israel we fall into doubt and unbelief and through punishment and repentance experience again God's help and faithfulness. All this is not mere reverie but holy, godly reality. We are torn out of our own existence and set down in the midst of the holy history of God on earth. There God dealt with us, and there He still deals with us, our needs and our sins, in judgment and grace. It is not that God is the spectator and sharer of our present life, howsoever important that is; but rather that we are the reverent listeners and participants in God's action in the sacred story.[1]

The Bible is not only a record of the words of God; the Bible *is* the Word of God—the "God-breathed" (2 Tim 3:16), "living and active" (Heb 4:12) Word of God. The Word that goes out from the mouth of the Lord does not return empty, but accomplishes what its Master desires (Is 55:11). When we are open to it, the Word absorbs our world, tears us out of our own existence and sets us down in the midst of godly reality. Exposure to the Word is always transformative. The axis on which our worlds turn is realigned and our compasses are reoriented. Henri de Lubac, S. J. (1896–1991) observes with some astonishment that in the Scriptures we find more than facts or morals or history—we find *ourselves*. "It is a living mirror, a living and efficacious Word, a sword penetrating at the juncture of soul and spirit, which makes our secret thoughts appear and reveals to us our heart."[2]

---

[1]Dietrich Bonhoeffer, *Life Together*, trans. John Doberstein (New York: Harper & Row, 1954), pp. 53-54.

[2]Henri de Lubac, *Medieval Exegesis*, trans. Mark Sebanc (Edinburgh: T & T Clark, 1998), 2:142.

Not only do we find our desires, hopes and failures laid bare, we also encounter the Author of all things—the face of God in the letter of the page. Augustine advises in one of his sermons: "let the Scriptures be the countenance of God."[3] As we listen to the words of Scripture, we find God, or rather, God finds and shows himself to us. The Bible is different than other books because *here* it is that in a most special way we step into the presence of the divine as the divine presence steps into us (Rev 3:20).

MODERN READING HABITS

Before we think specifically about the Bible and how to read it, it might be helpful first to think about how ordinary people approach and interpret texts in general. Despite what we said above about the uniqueness of the Bible, our tendency is to read the Bible like we read other books. So, the natural question is: how do we modern people read other books?

This question at first sounds very trifling and pedantic. But as it turns out, ordinary, everyday modern readers have very peculiar reading habits. Essentially, those reading habits are based on a referential theory of meaning. Words on paper mean what they refer to; the meaning of the word "tree" is its ability to refer to that tall green thing outside your window, the biography on Martin Luther is meaningful insofar as it accurately refers to facts about the person and times of Martin Luther. Likewise, when modern readers of the Bible ask, "What does this mean?" they are usually trying to ask, "To what do these words refer?" They want to know the historical context, the authorial intent and the original connotations of the words.

John O'Keefe and R. R. Reno, two associate professors of theology at Creighton University who combined their areas of expertise to study this issue, found that in modern methods of interpretation "the Bible has an *x*, a subject matter, and good interpretation helps readers shift attention from the signs or words to the *x* that is the real meaning of the

---

[3]Augustine *Sermon* 22, 7, quoted in Peter Brown, *Augustine of Hippo*, 2nd ed. (Berkeley: University of California Press, 2000), p. 259.

signs and words."[4] Once the reference is discovered, the meaning becomes clear and can be applied to the reader as needed. Indeed, this is the pattern of many typical sermons: an exposition of what the text originally *meant* through word studies and historical overviews, and then an *application* of that meaning to contemporary life. The meaning is extracted like ointment from the leaves of a plant and applied to the listener wherever needed. The biblical text, so it would seem, has only one meaning, its reference, but an infinite variety of applications. The text means this or that, but each person is free to "get" something different from it, depending on how they need it applied.

It should be noticed that between the original reference and contemporary application, there is no direct relationship. Once one has the precious *meaning* of the text, the text itself is no longer needed. It is up to the individual to decide how to utilize the meaning, and every individual might use it differently. Scripture becomes democratized and individualized. The best a pastor can do is to suggest possible uses or provide topical indices for self help: Feeling blue, look here; need courage, turn here.

This way of reading the Bible—looking for a single point of reference and a bonanza of individual applications—seems to most of us as a normal and ordinary process. According to O'Keefe and Reno, however, it is not. This way of reading Scripture is a relatively recent invention.

> Our [modern] views about the Bible's meaning were not held by premodern readers. Premodern readers assumed that events depicted in the Bible actually occurred as described, but surprisingly little of their interpretation depended on this assumption. They simply did not ask: "What is the event or truth to which the Bible refers?" . . . Scripture was for them the orienting, luminous center of a highly varied and complex reality, shaped by divine providence. It was true not by virtue of successfully or accurately representing any one event or part of this divinely ordained reality. Rather, the truth rested in the scripture's power to illuminate and disclose the order and pattern of all things.[5]

---

[4]John O'Keefe and R. R. Reno, *Sanctified Vision* (Baltimore, Md.: Johns Hopkins University Press, 2005), p. 9.
[5]O'Keefe and Reno, *Sanctified Vision*, p. 11.

The words of the Word speak divine revelation and shine forth the order and pattern of reality so as to draw us in and reorient us to what is really real. According to the third-century biblical scholar, defender of the faith and teacher of new converts, Origen of Alexandria, when one studies the Scriptures with due care and attention, "it is certain that in the very act of reading and diligently studying them his mind and feelings will be touched by a divine breath and he will recognize that the words he is reading are not utterances of man but the language of God."[6]

All Scripture, because it is the living Word of God as well as the historical words of humans, is "living and active" as Hebrews 4 says and works on us through the power of the Spirit. Origen spent his life with Scripture, compiling manuscripts and different editions, preaching, teaching and daily expounding passages before churches, small groups and individuals. He says that because Scripture is not only a product of human hands but was also "written by the Spirit of God," we should expect it to "have a meaning, not such only as is apparent at first sight, but also another, which escapes the notice of most. For those (words) which are written are the forms of certain mysteries, and the images of divine things."[7] The full meaning of Scripture with its "mysteries" and "images of divine things" cannot be captured by a flat explanation of the text's grammar and syntax, historical context and authorship. These strategies may all be helpful, interesting and even necessary, but they are only starting points and not the last word.[8]

READING RULES

"Let me venture, trusting in Him who commanded to search the Scriptures,"[9] to suggest that we read the Bible best when we read it *as Christians*, as disciples trying to emulate the faith, love, hope and justice of Jesus. The Bible is, after all, a religious book, a book of Christian

---

[6]Origen *De Principiis* 4.1.6, quoted in John O'Keefe and R. R. Reno, *Sanctified Vision* (Baltimore, Md.: Johns Hopkins University Press, 2005), p. 12.

[7]Origen *De Principiis* preface, ANF, vol. 4, p. 241.

[8]Karl Barth, *Epistle to the Romans*, trans. Edwyn Hoskyns (New York: Oxford University Press, 1968), pp. 16-17.

[9]Methodius *Banquet of the Ten Virgins*, discourse 8.4, ANF, vol. 6, p. 336.

revelation. Christ stands at the center of the biblical faith and message, all else must find its place under the shadow of the cross. The text is not a flat surface where all points are equal. To some, this statement may sound shocking and even heretical. But let me prove my point. Try this little experiment. Check to see if the women in your church refrain from attending worship service while menstruating. Does anyone in your church eat bacon and ham or have tattoos? Does anyone consistently practice the Sabbath laws about requiring rest from work? Do men uncover their heads in church and do women cover their heads with a scarf or their faces with a veil? If the good people of your church do not observe these regulations, they are in clear violation of laws laid down in Scripture. Some might respond, "Well, some of those prescriptions are no longer relevant to us and our culture." I would argue that the reason we set aside these prescriptions is *not* because they were culturally conditioned and therefore no longer relevant to us in the twenty-first century. It is not true to say that some parts of Scripture are culturally conditioned while others represent timeless truths.[10] All truths are situated in space and time, in contexts and cultures and languages. The criterion for interpretation and application is not culture but *Christ*; it is not what is historically relevant but what is christologically related.

The person of Christ brings everything into focus; he is situated at the pinnacle of Scripture, so that everything that comes before it points to Christ and everything that comes after it reflects back on Christ. "He is before all things, and in him all things hold together" (Col 1:17). The words on either side of the Word-made-flesh must be judged and valued in light of and in reference to that first and final Word. Colossians reminds us that "the mystery of God" is Christ himself, "in whom are hidden all the treasures of wisdom and knowledge" (Col 2:2-3).

How do we practice this conviction? How do we read Scripture with our eyes on Jesus? Early on, the Christian tradition observed four senses of meaning in the pages of Scripture. A little rhyming verse that circulated in late medieval times articulates the four senses this way:

---

[10]Richard Hays, *The Moral Vision of the New Testament* (New York: HarperCollins, 1996), p. 310.

Littera gesta docet,
quid credas allegoria,
Moralis quid agas,
quo tendas anagogia.

Which is to say,

The letter shows us what God and our fathers did;
The allegory shows us where our faith is hid;
The moral meaning gives us rules of daily life;
The anagogy shows us where we end our strife.[11]

For those unfamiliar with the idea of Scripture having four senses, the Jesuit scholar Henri de Lubac goes to painstaking lengths in his multivolume *Medieval Exegesis* to demonstrate the commonplace presence of this idea in patristic and medieval thinkers.[12] He aims to show that it is not a recent invention, but a very old way of talking about how Christians read God's holy Word. This was once the natural and normal way of engaging Holy Writ. More will be said about each of these senses in a moment, but it is worth pausing on the language of "senses" because it can be misleading. By "senses" we do not mean to say that the text has four distinct and different *meanings*, four main ideas or four things being communicated. Such misconceptions are clumsy and inaccurate. The Bible and its message form a single, unified whole. Because of its strong internal cohesion, it is able to permit various points of entry and various levels of understanding; in fact, it radiates a cornucopia of senses to those who will take the time and effort to see them. It is like a jewel which, when turned in the light, reveals different colors and faces and angles. One can find an endless variety of insights and entryways, depending on how one turns the jewel. The text opens itself in innumerable ways to the reader sensitive to the Spirit's prompting.

It must be made clear at the outset that finding multiple senses in the Bible does not mean disregarding or going against a straightforward reading of the text. The basic words of the text must always re-

---

[11]Henri de Lubac, *Theological Fragments*, trans. Rebecca Balinski (San Francisco: Ignatius, 1989), p. 109. Robert Grant, *A Short History of the Interpretation of the Bible*, rev. ed. (New York: Macmillan, 1972), p. 119.
[12]Henri de Lubac, *Medieval Exegesis*, 2 vols. (Grand Rapids: Eerdmans, 1998, 2000).

main in focus. As Thomas Aquinas states, the four senses of Scripture are "based on the literal, and presuppose it."[13] With brilliant subtlety, Aquinas explains,

> the senses [of Scripture] are not multiplied because one word signifies several things, but because the things signified by the words can be themselves signs of other things. Thus in Holy Scripture no confusion results, for all the senses are founded on one—the literal—from which alone can any argument be drawn.[14]

The unity of the biblical message is maintained in the very words of the text. But those words can be signs of more than one thing, they can connect and relate to other parts of Scripture, and they can invite deeper introspection and conviction.

St. Thomas does not intend to say that there are secret, hidden truths buried within the texts that only a select few can access, as if there were some "Bible code" to be cracked by the highly intellectual or super-spiritual. Instead, "nothing of Holy Scripture perishes because of this [i.e., the presence of multiple senses], since nothing necessary to faith is contained under the spiritual sense which is not elsewhere put forward clearly by the Scripture in the literal sense."[15] Every interpretation of Scripture must be based on the actual words of Scripture; the identification of the various senses must clarify, not obscure or depart from the text. Any reading of the Bible that cannot be supported by other passages or that is not true to the broader message of Scripture as a whole should be corrected in favor of clearer and more representative interpretations. Such a commitment to the integrity of the text does not limit meaning, but makes meaning possible.

JUSTICE

"The letter shows us what God and our fathers did." The "letter" is the historical or literal sense of the text that "shows us what God and our fathers did." It tells us what happened. Respecting the "letter" requires

---

[13]Thomas Aquinas *Summa Theologiae* 1.1.10.
[14]Ibid.
[15]Ibid.

the virtue of justice. We must read the Bible justly, fairly and rightly—that is, according to its letter. The Bible itself commands this! Justice is perhaps the most regularly reiterated command in the Bible. Again and again, we are admonished to love justice and practice righteousness.

In Old Testament passages like Genesis 18:19, Exodus 23:6, Deuteronomy 27:19, Psalm 37:28 and Micah 6:8, the quality of *mishpat*, Hebrew for "justice" or "righteousness," is extolled above all other laws and admonitions. Without fairness, honesty, integrity and the will to do the right thing, one cannot love God or neighbor. Only the person or nation that upholds justice and does what is fair, equitable and right can be called good and laudable. Indeed, *mishpat* is the characteristic most often attributed to God himself in the Hebrew Scriptures, as in Deuteronomy, "The Rock, his work is perfect, for all his ways are justice" (Deut 32:4); the Psalms, "He loves righteousness and justice; the earth is full of the steadfast love of the LORD" (Ps 33:5); and Isaiah, "The LORD is a God of justice" (Is 30:18). Consistently, God Almighty expects his people to also model this divine quality, "This is what the LORD says: 'Maintain justice and do what is right, for my salvation is close at hand and my righteousness will soon be revealed'" (Is 56:1). And in the Gospels, the theme of justice is carried forward in passages like Matthew 12:18-20 and Luke 11:42. Elsewhere in the New Testament, James warns the church about showing favoritism (Jas 2:1-13) and Revelation confirms that justice will be served in the end, when everyone will be "judged according to what they had done" (Rev 20:12).

It is right to start with the virtue of justice because, in many ways, it is the most universal and basic virtue, without which no other virtue can survive. Aristotle makes this same observation in a different but equally ancient setting when he says, "In justice is summed up the whole of virtue" and, "Justice, in this sense, then, is not a part of virtue but the whole of it."[16] Personal character begins and ends with justice.

Guided by *mishpat*, the first question we should ask when reading

---

[16]Aristotle *Nicomachean Ethics* 5.1, trans. J. A. K. Thomson (New York: Penguin Books, 2004), p. 115. There are, of course, differences between the Hebrew and the Aristotelean Greek conception of justice. What should be attended to here, however, is its antiquity and universality.

Scripture is: How should justice be done to the text? Good readers must start by taking the words and the events of the story seriously. "True exegesis involves, of course, much sweat and many groans."[17] We must allow the text to speak without imposing our preconceptions, judgments and desires upon it. We must first of all treat the letter of the text justly, which means not ignoring historical, critical and stylistic issues, but exploring them to the fullest. We treat the text with academic integrity not because of pressure from the guilds of higher learning, but for the sake of truth. Clement of Alexandria says, "I call him truly learned who brings everything to bear on the truth; so that from geometry, and music, and grammar, and philosophy itself, culling what is useful, he guards the faith against assault."[18] We are compelled by our Christian commitments to truth and justice more than by academic expectations or pride of intellect.[19]

Our task as Christian exegetes does not end when all the historical, cultural and grammatical tools have been employed on the text; rather, that is where it starts. For too many interpreters, the entire exposition of a passage is finished once the historical background and the linguistic issues have been addressed; for a Christian reading, it marks only the beginning. Understanding the letter of the text constitutes what Mortimer Adler calls an "elementary" step, even if a necessary one, in the interpretive process. There are many more jewels to be unearthed. Take for example the multiple ways that one swift leg motion can be described: as kicking a ball, scoring a goal, winning the game, capturing the World Cup, bringing glory to one's homeland.[20] The interpreter

---

[17]Barth, *Epistle to the Romans*, p. 17.
[18]Clement of Alexandria *The Stromata* 1.9, ANF, vol. 2, p. 310.
[19]Origen remarks,

> You who are accustomed to be present at the divine mysteries know how you receive the Lord's body with every care and reverence, lest the smallest crumb of the consecrated gift should be dropped. You would think, and think rightly, that you were culpable if something fell to the ground through your negligence. If you use, and rightly use, such care about his body, why do you think it less of a crime to be negligent about his word than his body? (Origen *Homily on Exodus* 13.3, Fathers of the Church, vol. 71 [Washington, D.C.: Catholic University of America Press, 1982])

[20]Kevin Vanhoozer, "Introduction," in *Everyday Theology*, ed. Kevin Vanhoozer, Charles Anderson and Michael Sleasman (Grand Rapids: Baker, 2007), p. 47.

must start with the elementary, literal act—putting one's foot into a soccer ball with force. But there are other, and arguably more important, meanings that the act has, like winning the World Cup. Just because we got the bare facts straight, that does not mean we have exhausted the meaning of the event, or the text.

Augustine pleads that we not be satisfied with just the bare facts. There is more than appears on the surface. What is at stake is our very being as Christians. When a person persists in misreading and undervaluing Scripture, they begin to harbor a certain displeasure with Scripture. "If he encourages this evil to spread it will be his downfall."[21] Because when this happens, faith begins to totter.

> And if faith falters, love itself decays. For if someone lapses in his faith, he inevitably lapses in his love as well, since he cannot love what he does not believe to be true. If on the other hand he both believes and loves, then by good conduct and by following the rules of good behaviour he gives himself reason to hope that he will attain what he loves. So there are these three things which all knowledge and prophecy serve: faith, hope, and love.[22]

FAITH

"The allegory shows us where our faith is hid." The second sense of the text is what we are calling the allegorical sense. Once the historical and contextual letter of the passage has been established, other dimensions can be considered. Most scholars get the shivers around the word "allegory." Allegory has become synonymous with wildly distorted interpretations and fantasies wrenched out of a few words. There have certainly been abuses. We can point to instances in which entire cults and radical movements have been launched on the basis of a far-fetched allegorical reading of Scripture. But the way to correct such abuses is not to abandon allegory all together or deny any deeper significance in the words. As the current Anglican Archbishop of Canterbury Rowan Williams observes,

---

[21]Augustine *On Christian Teaching* 1.37, trans. by R. P. H. Green (New York: Oxford University Press, 1997), p. 28.
[22]Ibid.

There is an insanity in which hidden connections are everything, in which the excess of symbolism becomes the habitual climate of thought; but there is equally an insanity in which excess is denied and the world reduced to that series of problems which my mind currently happens to engage.[23]

Yes, there is a danger of over-mystifying, but there is an equal danger of demystifying. If we have the courage to reclaim allegory from its misuses we will find that the idea is much less bizarre and otherworldly than it first appears. Its purpose is simply to show us "where our faith is hid." Rightfully understood, it describes how one reads the Scripture by the light of faith. Paul himself used the term "allegory" in his memorable illustration of law and grace (Gal 4:24). By his allegory he attempted to show that all Scripture speaks to faith.[24]

The Bible is a book of faith. In order to taste the wine stored in the cellars, it is necessary to pass through the gate and descend the stairs of faith.[25] To read it with the eyes of faith is to read it faithfully. Or, to borrow a metaphor from John O'Keefe and R. R. Reno, "allegorical interpretation reads a text as a map. The ordered reality of the text exists not for its own sake but for the sake of guiding our thoughts onto the topography of something else, something more real and more important."[26] Faith maps the way to truth in the scriptural landscape.

The question we must ask as we read with faith is: What should be believed? How does this text encourage, enrich or challenge faith? In some passages, it is obvious, like the letters of Paul. In others, not so much, like the sordid chronicles of the monarchy in 1 and 2 Kings or

---

[23]Rowan Williams, *Grace and Necessity: Reflections on Art and Love* (Harrisburg, Penn.: Morehouse, 2005), p. 141.

[24]"If the law, according to the apostle, is spiritual, containing the images 'of future good things,' come then, let us strip off the veil of the letter which is spread over it, and consider its naked and true meaning" (Methodius *Banquet of the Ten Virgins* discouse 5.7, ANF, vol. 6, p. 328).

[25]Lubac, *Medieval Exegesis*, 2:112-13. See David Grumett, *De Lubac: A Guide to the Perplexed* (New York: T & T Clark, 2007), p. 85.

[26]Reno and O'Keefe, *Sanctified Vision*, pp. 69-70. Although they do not use the word "allegory," this is perhaps what theologians like Hans Boersma, N. T. Wright and Colin Gunton (and others) mean when they speak of "metaphor." The concept of metaphor has taken on the theological role and interpretive function once assigned to allegory. Hans Boersma, *Violence, Hospitality, and the Cross* (Grand Rapids: Baker, 2004); N. T. Wright, *Christian Origins and the Question of God*, 3 vols. (Minneapolis: Fortress, 1992, 1996, 2003); Colin Gunton, *The Actuality of the Atonement* (Grand Rapids: Eerdmans, 1989).

the sultry romance of Song of Solomon. What lesson of faith can be learned from these? Even in instances where the element of faith is muted or seemingly negated, it is present.[27] The stories and interludes, confessions and prayers, prophecies and laws are all part of the grand narrative of God's people and God's own self. As Scripture unfolds this narrative it also unfolds and reveals God's very identity.

By reading this holy book through the eyes of faith we mean to enact Nicholas Lash's helpful principle: "God does not say many things, but one."[28] According to Lash, this is no arithmetical statement, for of course the Bible uses many words and tells many stories. Rather, it is a theological reading rule: "it tells you how to read the Scriptures."[29] The one thing that God says is his Word, "In the beginning was the Word, and the Word was with God and the Word was God" (Jn 1:1). Lash explains, "God speaks the one Word that God is and, in that one Word's utterance, all things come into being, find life and shape and history and, in due time, find fullest focus, form and flesh, in Mary's child."[30] Irenaeus of Lyons anticipated Lash's reading rule: "If any one, therefore, reads the Scriptures with attention, he will find in them an account of Christ."[31] Ultimately, all of Scripture testifies to the one Word which God has been uttering since before time.

LOVE

"The moral meaning gives us rules of daily life." The third sense of Scripture involves its "moral meaning," or tropological sense. As the text is reread, the question becomes: What *should* be done? This question might be answered in any number of ways by moral theorists—for instance, in terms of duties, rights, policies or consequences. When Christians ask what should be done, they are asking the question of love. What would love do?

Morality, for the disciple of Jesus, begins and ends with love; Jesus said to his disciples at the Passover meal on the climactic eve of his

---

[27]Augustine *On Christian Teaching* 1.2, pp. 8-9.
[28]Nicholas Lash, *Holiness, Speech, and Silence* (Burlington, Vt.: Ashgate, 2004), pp. 66-67.
[29]Ibid., p. 67.
[30]Ibid., p. 66.
[31]Irenaeus *Against Heresies* 4.26.1, ANF, vol. 1, p. 496.

arrest, "A new command I give you: Love one another. As I have loved you, so you must love one another. By this all men will know that you are my disciples, if you love one another" (Jn 13:34-35). As if that were not clear enough, he added, "If you love me, you will obey what I command" (Jn 14:15). He goes on to say, "My commandment is this: Love one another as I have loved you" (Jn 15:12). Paul extolled love as the "greatest" of the virtues in 1 Corinthians 13:13. John Chrysostom (347–407), the magnificent preacher from Constantinople—so magnificent in fact that listeners were warned not to bring money to church because they would become so enraptured by his message they would not notice the pick-pockets—declared that love is "the creator of every virtue" and that

> love is the great teacher. She has the power to free men from error, to form their minds, to take them by the hand and lead them on to wisdom. Yes, she may even make men out of stones. Do you want to find her power and know it? Bring me a man who is a coward, a man who is fearful at every noise and who trembles at shadows. Let him be violent, let him be rude, more of the brute than a man, let him be wanton and lustful, but deliver him into the hands of love, lead him into her school and you will soon see the coward change into a man of high spirit and of a fearless heart.[32]

Love, as the sum of all morality, must be at the heart of all Bible reading. In fact, regarding the text according to the virtue of love is precisely the method recommended by Jesus. We can imagine the scene told of in the Gospel of Matthew. Jesus has just silenced another pompous and over-privileged smart-aleck with his usual serene tone, which has an amazing ability of slicing his interlocutors to pieces. The crowd roars in delight to see the rug pulled out from underneath Jesus' opponent, a Sadducee. Just then, "an expert in the law" steps forward, his fingers inky with a hard morning's work of painstakingly copying the holy text, and taps one of the tightly rolled scrolls of the Torah. He asks, which one of its infinite commandments is the greatest. The crowd leans in. Jesus does not hesitate, but answers, "'Love the Lord

---

[32]John Chrysostom, "Homily on 1 Corinthians 13:4," NPNF, 1st series, vol. 12, p. 200.

your God with all your heart, and with all your soul, and with all your mind.' This is the first and greatest commandment. And the second is like it: 'Love your neighbor as yourself'" (Mt 22:37). Well and good. But let us not miss how Jesus ends his pronouncement, for he not only admonishes love for God and fellow human, he also makes it a reading rule: "All the Law and the Prophets hang on these two commandments" (Mt 22:40). That is to say, the law and the prophets, the Hebrew Scriptures, are bound together by love. Love works as a coat hook on which the Word is draped.

Once again, we turn to Augustine for comment. In the spring of 391, when young and spry Augustine arrived on his first visit to the ancient Roman seaside city of Hippo Regius, "Royal Port," he went to hear the local bishop, Valerius, preach. The aged bishop preached on the pressing needs of the church, including the need for more support of the priestly ministries. Taking him at his word, the congregation immediately looked around for someone to help Valerius. They found a God-send: a newcomer standing in the nave of the church, his arms folded lightly, innocently watching the proceedings. The unsuspecting Augustine was grabbed and thrust forward. Everything worked out according to bishop Valerius's plan, who knew how to spy and recruit good help, whether they were willingly or not. He ordained Augustine on the spot.[33] Augustine was made a priest of the North African church at Hippo. A few years later, when Valerius grew too old to perform his duties, Augustine was forced into yet another role: Valerius's replacement as bishop of Hippo. As bishop, he was immediately thrust into civil and ecclesial controversy. The church he had inherited was being slowly sawn in two by different factions, especially by a group known as the Donatists. Augustine strove hard to put out the fires and "defeat" the factions with sermons, open-air debates, intellectual treatises, edicts and even sing-song jingles. One treatise he began about this time was on Scripture and the *right* way to interpret it, as opposed to the Donatists and the other contentious dissenters, who *must* be interpreting Scripture wrongly because they

---

[33]Possidius tells the story in his early biography of Augustine, *Life of St. Augustine* 4.2, *Early Christian Biographies* (Washington: Catholic University of America, 1952), p. 77.

disagreed with Augustine. Why couldn't they just admit they were wrong and he was right?

More than ever Augustine needed a divine lamp of patience and love to order his steps. He needed the gentle Shepherd to remind him that if he read and interpreted the Scriptures in anger and spitefulness, he was sure to misread and misinterpret. For the time being, he put down his treatise on Scripture, knowing that he was not in a fit condition to write a book teaching others how to read it. He came back and finished the project much later, once he had learned something more about patience, humility and the virtue of love. "So anyone who thinks that he has understood the divine scriptures or any part of them, but cannot by his understanding build up this double love of God and neighbour, has not yet succeeded in understanding them."[34] Augustine had to admit that this exhortation included him. He had not spoken the truth in love to those who were, after all, his neighbors—the Donatists. Ephesians 4:15 orders us to speak the truth in love. When love vanishes, so does truth. If the virtue of love is not activated in our reading, truth will fail to communicate.

HOPE

Fourth, "the anagogy shows us where we end our strife." "Anagogy" is a transliteration of the Greek word for a "spiritual uplift" or mystical interpretation of a word or passage. Anagogically, one reads for the sake of hope. The virtue of hope is the will to see beyond the here and now, the choice to look beyond and above with confidence. In the book of Job we read, "you will be secure, because there is hope; you will look about you and take your rest in safety" (Job 11:18); and in Psalm 71, "For you have been my hope, O Sovereign Lord, my confidence since my youth" (Ps 71:5); and Paul said at his trial before the Sanhedrin, "I stand on trial because of my hope in the resurrection of the dead" (Acts 23:6).

Hope appears in over two hundred verses throughout the Bible. And yet, it is too often overlooked by theology. But the truth is that

---

[34]Augustine *On Christian Teaching* 1.36, p. 27.

the Christian faith is based on hope: hope of salvation, hope of resurrection, hope of final reconciliation. The resurrection of Jesus simultaneously produces history and punches through history. Our hope is on the other side of that hole in history. The resurrection event inaugurates the "new age" of forgiveness and peace. And although this new age is not yet fully realized it is very real. We witness to it by way of hope.

The reading question for the virtue of hope is simple: What should be hoped for? It is important to bear this question in mind as one encounters some of the bleak and tragic moments in the Hebrew Scriptures, like the story of Jephthah's daughter, the binding of Isaac, or the anguish of Lamentations that "The Lord has become like an enemy; he has destroyed Israel" (Lam 2:5 NRSV). The New Testament contains its own dark marks—Herod's slaughter of the innocent, the crucifixion of Christ and the death of Ananias and Sapphira. The visions of John of Patmos recorded in Revelation give a model of how to read God's Word and history through the lens of hope. The dominant message of Revelation is one of hope. We need to see past the graphic and bizarre episodes of cosmic confrontation and destruction, which, by the way, never result in repentance or change of heart (Rev 9:20-21), in order to encounter the promise stretched out of a "new heaven and a new earth."

> And I heard a loud voice from the throne saying, "Now the dwelling of God is with men, and he will live with them. They will be his people, and God himself will be with them and be their God. He will wipe every tear from their eyes. There will be no more death or mourning or crying or pain, for the old order of things has passed away." (Rev 21:3-4)

Christians live in anticipation of what is to come, eagerly awaiting the Day of the Lord, and, as importantly, the day after that Day. Christians should read the Bible with this hope at the forefront of their minds. Certainly the Gospel writers do, which might account for their tendency to see Old Testament prophecy in every act of Jesus, or better, to see in Jesus all of the Old Testament brought together. For the Gospel writers, every detail of Jesus' life corresponds to the divine narrative, from his place and manner of birth, his adolescence in Nazareth, the presence of John the Baptizer, his entry into Jerusalem on a donkey, the casting of lots for his clothes at the crucifixion and so on. When viewed disconnectedly and individually, certain Old Testament passages like that found in Isaiah 7, "The virgin will be with child and will give birth to a son" (Is 7:14), do not appear to refer directly to Mary. How could they, having been written hundreds of years before Mary lived? However, under the guidance of the Spirit, the Gospel writers saw rightly that they do. But for the Gospel writers, the Word of God was not divided and compartmentalized, and neither should it be for us. Cyril of Jerusalem affirms: "everything that concerns Christ has been written; there is nothing doubtful, since nothing is unattested. All has been inscribed in prophetic records, clearly written, not on tablets of stone, but by the Holy Spirit."[35]

The words of the text are not on a two dimensional surface, but a three dimensional one, like a tent or a pyramid, where all lines are drawn upward toward the incarnation of the Word. The dietary laws of Leviticus simply do not carry the weight of the Sermon on the Mount. All must be measured according to the standard of Christ, who is Lord of all, even of the text. Seeing the crucified One step out from the misty and mountainous forest of Scripture is, if we dare, an act of hope.

---

[35]He continues,

> You have heard the Gospel's account of the deeds of Judas; ought you not to receive testimony of this? You have heard that His side was pierced by a spear; should you not see whether this also is written? You have heard that He was crucified in a garden; ought you not to see if this is written? You have heard that He was sold for thirty pieces of silver; should you not learn what prophet said this? You have heard that He was given vinegar to drink; learn where even this is written. You have heard that His body was laid in a rock, and a stone placed thereon; should you not get testimony of this also from the prophet? You have heard that He was buried; should you not see whether the circumstances of His burial were written down accurately? You have heard that He rose again; should you not see whether we are mocking you in teaching all this? (Cyril of Jerusalem *Catechesis* 13.8, in *The Works of Saint Cyril of Jerusalem*, vol. 2, trans. Leo McCauley and Anthony Stephenson, The Fathers of the Church [Washington, D.C.: Catholic University of America Press, 1970], pp. 9-10)

UNITY

We are ready now to put the four senses together into a total package. The approach can be summarized as follows:

Category	Question	Virtue
Historical	What should you know in the text?	Justice
Allegorical	What should you believe?	Faith
Tropological	What should you do?	Love
Anagogical	What should you hope for?	Hope

"And now these three remain: faith, hope, and love" (1 Cor 13:13), and to these we add the undergirding virtue of justice, without which the others cannot stand (Is 54:1). "All of divine Scripture turns on these four wheels," said Dom Jean Leclercq.[36] The recognition of these multiple layers or depths of the divine Word means, as Henri de Lubac so beautifully writes, that

> Scripture is like the world: "undecipherable in its fullness and in the multiplicity of its meanings." A deep forest, with innumerable branches, "an infinite forest of meanings": the more involved one gets in it, the more one discovers that it is impossible to explore it right to the end. It is a table arranged by Wisdom, laden with food, where the unfathomable divinity of the Savior is itself offered as nourishment to all. Treasure of the Holy Spirit, whose riches are as infinite as himself. True labyrinth. Deep heavens, unfathomable abyss. Vast sea, where there is endless voyaging "with all sails set." Ocean of mystery.[37]

There is a depth and breadth to the holy Word yet to be discovered. It is amazing that de Lubac remained throughout his life awed and enthralled by the labyrinth and treasure of Scripture, especially since he experienced firsthand all the turmoil and petty politics of church life. He was censured by Pope Pius XII and accused of misrepresenting the faith by Roman Catholic colleagues. Eventually he was vindicated by the Second Vatican Council and, in his old age, made a cardinal. He saw the best and the worst in his fellow Christians. Even so, he remained captive to the Word of God, with its deep forests and delectable foods.

---

[36]Lubac, *Medieval Exegesis*, vol. 1, p. 73.
[37]Ibid., vol. 1, p. 75.

Realization of the richness of Scripture became a turning point in the life of St. Augustine of Hippo. It marked the beginning of his conversion to Christianity. Augustine was greatly confused and troubled at first by what he read in this strange book. He wondered how it could speak anthropomorphically about God (assigning to God hands, eyes and a sense of smell) and yet affirm God as spirit. He struggled to understand how some biblical patriarchs "who had several wives at the same time and killed people and offered animals in sacrifice" could be considered righteous.[38] Eventually Augustine came into contact with St. Ambrose of Milan (337–397), where he "heard first one, then another, then many difficult passages in the Old Testament Scriptures figuratively interpreted, where I, by taking them literally, had found them to kill (2 Cor 3:6)."[39] The biblical message is best served when it is handled not with flat and literalistic expectations, but with a genuine openness to the movement and leadership of the Spirit of Christ.

TEST CASE

As a test case for the rules to our game, our method of the four senses, let us take this passage from Matthew 12:

> Then some of the Pharisees and teachers of the law said to him, "Teacher, we want to see a miraculous sign from you." He answered, "A wicked and adulterous generation asks for a miraculous sign! But none will be given it except the sign of the prophet Jonah. For as Jonah was three days and three nights in the belly of a huge fish, so the Son of Man will be three days and three nights in the heart of the earth. The men of Nineveh will stand up at the judgment with this generation and condemn it; for they repented at the preaching of Jonah, and now one greater than Jonah is here." (Mt 12:38-41)

Justice. This is a complex episode with multiple textual layers. Doing justice to the text means identifying the main characters, actions and elements of the passage. First of all, who is this Jesus who is being addressed and then speaking? Who are the Pharisees and teachers and

---

[38]Augustine *Confessions* 3.7, translated by Henry Chadwick (New York: Oxford University Press, 1991), p. 43.
[39]Ibid., 5.14, p. 88.

what is their relation to Jesus? We might read other episodes to get a better feeling for how Jesus interacts with the Pharisees and teachers in general. Profitable interpretation also hinges on our understanding of the "sign" that is requested by the Pharisees. What did they expect? What would count as a sign? Jesus' response to the request involves a complicated allusion to the Old Testament story of Jonah. Doing justice to the text involves an explanation of this allusion. Jesus makes clear that the sign is between the three days Jonah spent in the belly of the sea monster and the three days the Son of Man will be in the heart of the earth, in the grave.[40] The immediate audience, including Jesus' own disciples, could not possibly have known what to make of this sign until after the resurrection. Jesus does not pause to explain his meaning to the scribes and Pharisees, but ends by chastising his listeners for not recognizing that someone "greater than Jonah" was among them.

Justly reckoned, this passage presents a short episode in which Jesus' authority is challenged by the religious elite. As he does in similar instances, Jesus turns the challenge on its head and uses the opportunity to teach about his own mission.

Faith. Reading with the eyes of faith, we are cut to the quick by Jesus' accusation that "a wicked and adulterous generation asks for a miraculous sign." We know that the adulterous generation includes us. Our adultery is our lusting after entertainment instead of calling, commercial appeasement instead of commitment, a sign instead of an encounter with the living God. We greedily expect signs from God; we want signs about our love lives, signs for our career decisions, signs that God cares or knows or whatever. Jesus reins in our stray hearts and directs us to the ultimate sign of God's concern and desire: the suffering and death of the Son of God at the hands of humans. Who do you say that I am? As Jonah's confinement in the belly of the whale was not as much a punishment as a rescue from death—remember he had been thrown overboard to drown in the briny water when the sea creature snags him—so Christ's surrender to death for three days does not represent the punishment of God as much as God's salvation and rescue.

---

[40]On Jonah, see Jack Sasson, *Jonah*, Anchor Bible 24B (New York: Doubleday, 1990).

The salvation and rescue is complete when the grave spit out its contents—Christ raised from death. And so, our faith is directed to the resurrected Lord.

Love. Moving from the question of faith to love, we learn that the labor of love is easily distracted by signs and spectacles. We must be about the business at hand, working as laborers in the vineyard so that when the master returns, Nineveh will not stand up in judgment of us. In addition to this warning, we catch a glimpse of the workings of love by contrasting Jonah and Jesus. Jonah's whale predicament resulted from his own disobedience—he landed in the belly of the whale because he ran away from God's call to Nineveh. By contrast, Jesus foresaw his own sufferings and embraced them as God's will. Disciples are called to obey, even as Jesus does, and not to avoid. Jesus sets the pattern for how to respond to God's will. We genuinely love when we respond as Jesus, and we must live in hope that God's Spirit will so help us.

Hope. Finally we come to the virtue of hope. The sense of hope in this passage is the anticipation of resurrection. As the sea monster spit Jonah out onto the sandy beach after three days, so the grave spit out Jesus. Death could not hold this one. Jesus had not merely lived and then died, he *was* life. If we have this life living in us, then we too are assured that death will not hold our bodies forever. We have reason to hope that we too will join our Master in resurrection. "Just as Christ was raised from the dead by the glory of the Father, so we too might walk in the newness of life . . . [and] be united with him in a resurrection like his" (Rom 6:4-5 NRSV). Despite this promise, we are sobered by Jesus' warning that at the judgment, even Nineveh will rise up against those of us who refuse to hear the Word and properly honor Jesus as the Christ.

In my own reading of Matthew 12, the meaning of the text was not extracted with a syringe and then applied as needed to relevant life issues. Rather, the story draws us in and refigures our needs and issues according to its vision and its virtues. Undoubtedly, Matthew 12:39-41 contains additional insights I have overlooked. As long as the text is treated justly, faithfully, lovingly and hopefully, any number of avenues might be explored. As John Chrysostom understood, it is impossible to "overread" the Bible. "For, just as with grains of incense, the more they are moved about with your fingers, the greater the fragrance they give out," he says in a homily, "so it is with the Scriptures in our experience; the more you devote to studying them, the more you are able to discover the treasure hidden in them, and thereby gain great and unspeakable wealth."[41] This being said, the text cannot be forced to mean *whatever* the reader wants. Justice will not allow that. The interpretation is directed and limited by the theological virtues, as exemplified most perfectly by the life, death and resurrection of Jesus.

Jesus himself exemplifies how to handle the text, appropriating the story of Jonah for the purpose of foreshadowing his own death and resurrection. It is possible to maintain the integrity of the story of Jonah in its historical and pre-Christian setting, while at the same time acknowledging that the Word of God cuts through space and time and is not bound to only one historical intention. If Jesus of Nazareth most fully reveals the eternal and unified Word of God, then Jonah, *and every other book in the Bible*, both in the Old and New Testament, must be reoriented toward that Word. All words must be gathered together under the shadow of the cross. All roads lead to Bethlehem. All Scripture finds its fulfillment in the one who "summed up in Himself the whole human race from the beginning to the end."[42]

Observing the four senses of Scripture is not meant to impose laws rigidly to be followed. These are virtues to be lived. We are not required to go through a checklist of justice, faith, love and so forth every time we open the Bible, although the process might be a good discipline to follow. The point is that if we are maturing disciples, then every time we open the Bible and read, we do so with these virtues and aims in mind. That is to say, in order to read the text properly, we must read it virtuously, righteously, Christianly. We read the Christian Scriptures best when we read them *as Christians*, as disciples trying to emulate the faith, love, hope and justice of Jesus.

---

[41]John Chrysostom *On Romans* 7.2, NPNF, 1st series, vol. 2, pp. 416-27.
[42]Irenaeus *Against Heresies* 5.23.2, ANF, vol. 1, p. 551.

CHRISTIANITY

AS CULTURE

CHRISTIANITY AS CULTURE

Happy are the people whose God is the LORD.

PSALM 144:15

IN OUR ANALOGY OF THE GAME, we peered from a distance at the players, those charged with handling the equipment correctly, playing by the rules, seeking the right goals and so forth. But can we get a closer look? What is the makeup of this team? How does one get "on the team"? What other expectations are there of players both on and off the field? To answer these questions and more, we must once again change analogies: from games to cultures. We have traveled with the image of the game as far as it will take us. Just as we left behind the other analogies, so we must now leave this one and board a new comparison.

"But you are a chosen people, a royal priesthood, a holy nation, a people belonging to God, that you may declare the praises of him who called you out of darkness into his wonderful light" (1 Pet 2:9). In this memorable verse, the author of 1 Peter speaks words of confidence and conviction to a fragile community of young believers rocked by the first outbreaks of imperial persecution. He encourages them to keep hope in this "fiery ordeal" (1 Pet 4:12), praising them as the chosen race of Israel, a priestly caste and a nation ordained for a purpose. The Christ-followers addressed here are like a brave new counterculture. In many ways, as Peter indicates, Christianity functions like a culture. The comparison is a good and natural one. But in order to give more precision to the analogy, we must first say some words about what a culture is.

IDENTIFYING CULTURE

Raymond Williams (1921–1988) notes in his classic inquiry into various societal keywords that *culture* is "one of the two or three most complicated words in the English language."[1] Williams himself embodied some of these complications—he was a drama and literary critic who also wrote plays and novels, a television commentator who also produced TV shows, a Cambridge professor who never became too educated for his Welsh roots. It would be difficult indeed to say in a word which culture defined Williams as a person or what effect he had on culture as a whole.

The meanings, applications and implications of the word *culture* continue to shift as rapidly as the scenery in Times Square, so that anthropologists, social critics, politicians and sociologists are obliged to pour out considerable amounts of ink on the subject. In an attempt to rinse off some of the smudges of excess verbage, Kathryn Tanner, professor of theology at the University of Chicago's Divinity School, has written a very helpful study of *culture, Theories of Culture.*[2]

She says that in modern parlance *culture* has come to represent a universal category: a way of life. Any people group can lay claim to a particular way of life, and so every people group can claim a culture. All humans in community partake in culture, and most of them in multiple cultures. By *culture* Tanner is not trying to distinguish high culture from low culture or people who have culture from those who do not. Judgments of this type are prejudicial, mean-spirited and exclusionist. All people have culture—or to put it better, all people live and move and have being in cultural contexts. Most people's lives intertwine with multiple cultures. It is rarely something we choose and never something we possess exclusively.

---

[1]Raymond Williams, *Keywords* (London: Fontana, 1983), p. 87.
[2]Kathryn Tanner, *Theories of Culture: A New Agenda for Theology* (Minneapolis: Fortress, 1997), pp. 25-28.

Culture affects all people. All people have peculiar ways of marrying, burying, celebrating, condemning, greeting, exchanging, working and resting. These practices vary from social group to social group. Patterns of behavior are precisely what differentiate one society from another. Culture incorporates an entire way of life and that way of living shapes individuals in the community as it is also shaped by the community and its history.

Culture is always formative and always being formed, always shaping lives but also adapting itself to lives. It is inclusive of all human practices and traditions and yet differs from group to group. Indeed, "it seems less and less plausible to presume that cultures are self-contained and clearly bounded units, internally consistent and unified wholes of beliefs and values simply transmitted to every member of their respective groups as principles of social order."[3] The more sociologists attend to it, the more difficult it is to nail down exactly what it is and where it starts and stops.

We know this from our experience in the Christian movement: there is no such thing as a unified, agreed upon, coherent "Christian culture." There are multiple forms of Christian culture(s). We could identify Baptists, Methodists, Pentecostals, Catholics, Greek Orthodox, Coptic, Messianic, ad infinitum. Even within a group like the Baptists, there exists a wide variety of subgroups, denominations and identities. Not all Baptists agree on what it means to be Baptist. This ambiguous, loose and even contradictory variety is a source of great consternation to all involved, and especially to anthropologists and sociologists trying to make generalizations.

Two obvious identifiers of culture are (1) common *knowledge* of the defining characteristics of a culture and (2) common *consensus* about those characteristics. There should be an understanding and agreement over what distinguishes one group from another, so it would seem. Surprisingly, in practice these two conditions are oftentimes absent. What is commonly presumed may not be so common. Some communities and traditions operate without knowledge or much consensus. Adherents

---

[3]Ibid., p. 38.

are sometimes completely unaware of their own heritage and inheritance and in perpetual disagreement over that heritage.

Cultures are unfinished conversations, ongoing processes, open questions and matters of lively debate, not mausoleums or antiquarian oddities. These are things we actively participate in, passionately discuss, learn about and give shape to.

There is a hidden danger here, though. If we permit such categorical looseness to permeate our conception of culture, what prevents us from saying that "culture" names nothing more than an aggregation of individuals who share anything at all in common? Culture, in this extrawide sense, does not define a purposeful and self-aware social entity—like an auto-labor union, the wood-crafts guild or a Benedictine abbey—rather it identifies those characteristics common to any random collection of individuals. What they share is not some greater social identity; culture, so it might seem, is limited to what individual constituents happen to have in common. Certain individuals share movie preferences, food tastes, income levels, zip codes, age-brackets, team-loyalties and so aggregately and accidently form a culture. It is culture by coincidence.

What prevents the term that once described a "way of life" from becoming a completely artificial and transitory category—youth culture, pop culture, gang culture, *Star Wars* culture, senior adult culture, rural culture, urban culture? The word can be used simply to group random market segments together in order to find patterns: to identify political leanings, educational trends, purchasing preferences, religious diversity, etc. An economic forecaster might try to predict what type of vehicle would appeal to a member of the college-graduated, family-oriented, median-income, thirty-something culture. Such an individual could be charted and grouped with others in a subset niche of the market. Everything can be turned into a statistic, and every statistic can be accounted for as a "culture" or "subculture."

The temptation is to mass produce and apply the label. Clearly, though, "culture" should name more than a demographic. There are limits to what actually constitutes and describes a people group. How might we better specify the circumference of culture? How might we give it shape and form, so as to be intellectually usable? Raymond Williams observes that the Latin root *colere*, from which "culture" is derived, has produced several distinct but related words. Besides "culture," *colere* spawned the words "colony," "cultivation" and "cult."[4] We must make an immediate disclaimer about the word "cult." It is a word derived from the root *colere*, and it originally meant to honor and worship. Today, "cult" carries primarily negative and derogatory connotations. It no longer means simply to honor or worship; mentioning the word "cult" makes people cringe and slowly back away as images of the Branch Davidians or the Solar Temple incident come to mind. I do not intend to debate or challenge the fact that this word has come to have creepy connotations—it is the natural course of words to evolve and change meanings—I want only to point out that culture is linguistically associated with the idea of worshiping, valuing and honoring.[5] The concept of "culture" rightfully enjoys all the senses of its derivative words: to honor with worship, to colonize or inhabit, and to cultivate or plant and nurture. The Christian faith can be compared to a culture in the sense that it too involves worship, colonies and cultivation.

SIMILARITIES AND DISSIMILARITIES

✚ Christianity bears resemblance to culture in that both offer very specific and special ways of valuing things. Both uphold certain moral values. Both are organized around peculiar expectations of honor, respect, appreciation and worship. Cultures survive by maintaining moral values and respected traditions. Christianity likewise demands the worship of the true God just as it fosters appreciation of certain goods, truths and morals.

✚ Christianity is like a culture in that both are ways of life. Christian-

---

[4]Williams, *Keywords*, p. 87.

[5]See Rodney Stark and William Bainbridge, *A Theory of Religion* (New York: Peter Land, 1987). The word *cult* is still used in a more neutral sense by academics in the study of religion to indicate worship rituals and their sociological practices. I distinctly remember a Sunday school class in which one of the class members, a Ph.D. student, repeatedly used the word *cult* to describe the ancient Israelites' worship of God. I watched the rest of the class as they listened—their eyes grew wide and their mouths dropped open. I quickly interrupted my friend and explained that he meant no disrespect to the Old Testament Israelites.

ity is more than a system of belief, or a religion, or even a worldview; it is a way of life. More than that, both Christianity and culture present ways of living *in community*. Culture is not meant to be lived alone, and neither is Christianity. Culture describes only groups or colonies of people, not single individuals.

✛ Christians are matured in the faith the same way that people are matured in the traditions and values of a culture—by a slow process of education and example. Culture is not an instantaneous thing, neither is Christianity. It takes formation, patience and the help of others. It must be cultivated.

In many ways Christianity looks and behaves like a culture. Shortly, we will consider in greater depth the various features of cultures and culture-making and show how Christianity incorporates and embodies them. Before we do so, however, we must point out some ways in which Christianity is *not* like a culture. Culture is a wonderful model for understanding how the Christian faith operates, but, like the other models we have looked at, it suffers from various limitations. It is not the perfect analogy for the following reasons:

▬ First, the analogy fails when it is used to exclude and alienate people. Care must be taken to avoid the impression that "Christian culture" is something separate from and alien to other cultures, peoples, or society as a whole. There sometimes emerges an "in" group and an "out" group, those who have culture and those who don't. Sometimes the idea of "Christian culture" seems to imply that Christians live detached from or above the world. The truth is that Christianity has never existed as a self-sufficient and independent culture.[6] It does not form a bubble of protection around its adherents, shielding them from the mean world out there. Rather, Christianity has always borrowed from, relied upon and contributed to all kinds of social practices, customs and technologies. People who identify themselves as Christians live their lives across many cultures and in multiple spheres. They belong to different ethnicities, nationalities, professional guilds, etc. Christian culture should

---

[6]Tanner, *Theories of Culture*, pp. 113-16.

not be conceived as a free-standing bubble, apart from all the other obligations and interests.

■ Second, the analogy fails when it is used to prop up idyllic, utopian fairytales. It sometimes happens that "Christian culture" becomes a political watchword, a denominational bludgeon, or a pastor's wish-dream. Sometimes pastors and pundits use "Christian culture" as a synonym for everything "good" Christians should be in favor of and should vote for, such that they might say, "Legislative bill X should be opposed because it goes against the Christian culture of our common Christian heritage." It is somewhat false to talk about *the* Christian culture, as if such a thing can be found in the ordinary world outside the theologian's laboratory.

■ Third, by comparing itself to culture, the practice of Christianity becomes subject to the criticisms of cultural relativism. Broadly speaking, cultural relativism argues that since ethical standards and norms differ from one culture to another and since ethical standards and norms depend upon cultural acceptance and adherence, then it must be the case that what is considered morally right and good depends upon the culture. There is no universal ethic that applies everywhere to everyone. Morality is a product of culture; people decide and enforce the rules they want and agree upon. Some cultures accept homosexuality, others reject it as immoral; some do not blink an eye at alcohol, others outlaw it; some expect women to wear long dresses and veils that cover their faces, others are shocked by such "repressive" expectations. If Christianity is a culture, then the validity of its truth-claims are all relative to its status as a culture. Christian culture claims certain things to be true about God, the universe and life. A relativist would say those things are only "true" insofar as believers accept them to be true and act on them. If Christians stopped believing them or acting on them, then they would no longer be true for the Christian culture. The way to answer this suggestion is to point to the failure of the analogy. The criticism only works when we assume an over-stretched analogy. That is to say, the criticism loses its force once we respect the limits of the analogy between Christianity and culture. It is readily affirmed that

Christian truths are not dependent upon their acceptance by believers, they are dependent upon God's revelation.

■ Fourth, the term *culture* is sometimes subject to certain stereotypes and misunderstandings that are not very helpful. For instance, to call someone a "cultural Christian" is not a compliment. "Cultural Christianity" is a pejorative phrase, describing a lukewarm, mediocre affinity for the Christian heritage and vaguely biblical values. The cultural Christian darkens the doors of the church at Christmas and Easter, and maybe offers a blessing before a big meal—but that is the extent of the commitment. If we are going to compare Christianity to a culture, we must be sure to clarify: we are not advocating cultural Christianity, but a much more robust understanding of culture and of Christian discipleship.

CHRISTIANITY AS CULTURE

THE WORSHIPING COLONY

Now that we have presented the points of likeness and unlikeness, we can begin to assess the real value of the comparison between culture and Christianity. In this chapter, I intend to draw out the comparison by examining the ways Christianity conducts worship and operates like a colony. In the next chapter, we will consider how it cultivates its disciples.

WORSHIP

Culture is lexically linked to cult; I would argue that the ancients who first made that connection in their language got something right. If you want to know what makes a civilization tick, find out what it values and honors. What does it worship? To what does it submit itself? Stanley Hauerwas and William Willimon, former colleagues at Duke University, observe, "Modern people like to think that as we become more educated, liberal, enlightened, the less we need to worship gods. No. We appear to have been created to worship, and worship something we will."[1] Whether it be the fates, the flag or the farm, we put our hope and trust in something. "The Bible never asks, 'Is there a God?' Rather, the Bible question is, '*Who* is the God who is there?'"[2]

If it is true that all people worship something and worship is about

---

[1]Stanley Hauerwas and William Willimon, *The Truth About God* (Nashville: Abingdon, 1999), p. 36.
[2]Ibid., p. 28.

what a group values, venerates and places ahead of everything else, then worship cannot be reduced to private devotion or Sunday morning ritual. It may involve that, but to be more exact, worship expresses what we as a people believe most deeply and what we believe most deeply directs our hearts.

To some practitioners and observers of Christianity, worship means nothing more than having a religious experience, by which they mean to say that worship can be reduced to an emotional high, a cathartic cleansing, a psychological release. It is about the rush of adrenaline when singing or the soothing calm of praying. I would certainly not deny that the emotive elements are important, even essential, but worship must be something more than simply an experience. Emotions change, experiences can be manipulated, misunderstood or blown out of proportion. Worship is not as transient as our emotions.

Worship involves the whole self. In worship we return the *whole self* to God. Because worship incorporates the entirety of one's being, it is *performative*. *Worship* is more than an action verb, it is a performative action verb like *promise* and *pledge* and *believe*. "I promise to love, honor and cherish in sickness and in health"; "I pledge allegiance"; "I believe in God"—these statements not only *say* something, they *do* something.[3] When I say I worship the God of the Lord Jesus, I am performing an act of faith; I am enacting what I announce (Num 30:2; Rom 10:9). Worship involves confession with the lips, baptism of the body, bowing of the head in prayer, a full surrender of the self.[4]

Worship is an action word. "The man bowed down and worshiped the LORD" (Gen 24:26); "Then they bowed down and worshiped" (Ex 12:27); "They all stood and worshiped" (Ex 33:10); "and they bowed their heads and worshiped the LORD with their faces to the ground" (Neh 8:6); "Come, let us bow down and worship, let us kneel before the

---

[3]Nicholas Lash, *Believing Three Ways in One God* (Notre Dame, Ind.: University of Notre Dame Press, 1992), p. 18. Also see George Lindbeck, *The Nature of Doctrine* (Philadelphia: Westminster Press, 1984), p. 64.

[4]See Cyril of Jerusalem *Mystagogical Lecture* 5, Fathers of the Church, vol. 64, pp. 191-203 for detailed description of the early church's liturgy and worship pattern, how they washed their hands, greeted one another with a holy kiss, bowed before the Lord, recited prayers and praises together.

Lᴏʀᴅ, our Maker!" (Ps 95:6); "My mouth will speak in praise of the Lord" (Ps 145:21); "praise him with tambourine and dancing, praise him with the strings and flutes" (Ps 150:4); "offer your bodies as a living sacrifice, holy and pleasing to God—this is your spiritual act of worship" (Rom 12:1); "they fell down on their faces before the throne and worshiped God" (Rev 7:11).

More than words, more than pious thoughts, more than goosepimples on the arm, more than a stirring in the heart, worship is a full-bodied way of living. It is at the heart of Christian culture. Lactantius (c. 250–325) had the task of instructing his fellow Roman citizens, especially in the top echelons of society (he knew Emperor Constantine and tutored his son), in the ways of the recently legalized Christian religion. This must have been exceptionally daunting, given the deep-seated generational habits of Roman paganism. Lactantius spent much of his massive tome, *Divine Institutes*, contrasting what the Romans, Greeks and pagans *supposed* to be true with what the God of Jesus Christ *revealed* to be true. On the subject of worship, he says,

> it is the duty of man, and in that one object the sum of all things and the whole course of a happy life consists, since we were fashioned and received the breath of life from Him on this account, not that we might behold the heaven and the sun, as Anaxagoras supposed, but that we might with pure and uncorrupted mind worship Him who made the sun and the heaven.[5]

Submission to the true God is the duty of humankind, the sum of all things and the path to happiness and fulfillment. It is why we were created.

Worship *expresses* culture, *enacts* culture and *makes* culture.[6] It does the work of culture by shaping habits, informing opinions, instilling values and giving us a place to stand within community before God. It is the ultimate act of cultural appreciation. Worship weans us from our idolatries and encourages us to appreciate those things that are of eternal value.

---

[5]Lactantius *Divine Institutes* book 6.1, ANF, vol. 7, p. 162.
[6]See Andy Crouch, *Culture Making: Recovering Our Creative Calling* (Downers Grove, Ill.: InterVarsity Press, 2008).

COLONIES

Not only is Christianity a culture in the sense that it involves worship, honor and conviction, it is a pattern of life to be enacted in real time. Christianity is lived in colonies. Colony, another derivative of the root word *colere*, is a fitting description of the Christian experience three reasons.

First, "colony" identifies a *real location*, not a lofty realm of spirits. A colony is a place to be inhabited. That sounds self-evident, but it needs to be said. The local church building is the primary place where this happens for Christians. For too many of us, it should be confessed, church is "just a place" to be frequented once a week, once a month or once every six months. In truth, church must be more than just a place. Indeed, it must be more than a quiet sanctuary into which we tread lightly for rest and contemplation. It must also be a hornet's nest of activity, life and community. We should note that the church building is not the only location available for gathering. There are other important "places" where like-minded believers find each other, network, pray and encounter—small groups that meet in homes, emergent cohorts, Theology-on-Tap gatherings and, yes, even online communities, blogs and Facebook pages. Many of these new ways have yielded delightful harvests. We must always be open to new ways of connecting as long as we do not lose sight of the importance of the connections, the importance of interpersonal encounters and accountability.

Second, the kind of location "colony" calls to mind is a *provisional* one. A colony is an outpost that has a footing but is not yet fully established. By definition it exists at a remove from its originating home. The classic biblical text Hebrews 11 paints the ancestors of the faith, like Abraham, Isaac, Jacob and Moses as "strangers and foreigners on the earth" who maintained settlements but never settled. These heroes of the Bible model for us the way of Diaspora, the dispersed and pilgrim people of God. This world in its present condition is not our home. We who follow Christ "are seeking a homeland" and "a better country, that is, a heavenly one," a city prepared by God (Heb 11:14-16). Augustine comments, "for as long as [the Christian] is in this mortal body, he is a pilgrim, far from the Lord; and so he walks by faith, not by sight. That is why he refers all peace, whether of body or of soul, or of both, to that peace which mortal man has with the immortal God, so that he may exhibit an ordered obedience, in faith, to the eternal Law."[7]

Colonies are always provisional and transitional. Not only is this world not our home, the work we do is not our own. We are called to do God's work (Mt 12:50). This means we may not be the ones to see that work to completion. We may die in faith, leaving the work uncompleted. "All these people were still living by faith when they died. They did not receive the things promised; they only saw them and welcomed them from a distance" (Heb 11:13). Risk and danger are close companions to colonization. God's call is always into the unknown, the unseen and the unexpected. "He put a new song in my mouth" (Ps 40:3).

Third, colonization implies exploration and *expansion*. Christianity has a universal vision; it is always exploring and expanding "to the ends of the earth" (Acts 1:8). Christians are obligated by Jesus himself to seek out those who do not know the gospel and share with them the faith we hold. The church that does not welcome newcomers cannot legitimately call itself a church (Acts 15:19). More than welcoming, believers are commanded to actively recruit. Sharing the faith and inviting others to join have always been central features and perennial tasks of Christianity. Other duties, benefits or expectations should not distract us from the fact that colonization remains our perennial task.

A WORD OF CAUTION

Unfortunately, "colonization" usually goes hand in hand with "colonialism." Christian missionaries of the past too often brought with them not only the liberating news of Christ, but also the constricting power of institutional control and cultural prejudice. Power is a temptation that preys upon all human flesh. The establishment of a colony necessarily requires the establishment of law and order, institution and authority. It is tempting to expand the need for order and authority into a grab for imperial power and prestige. When we share the gospel, we

---

[7]Augustine *City of God* 19.14, trans. by R. W. Dyson (New York: Cambridge University Press, 1998), p. 941.

must be careful that it is the gospel of Jesus Christ and not the gospel of my own ego. When our colonizing efforts take the form of colonialism, everyone loses.

Pope Gregory I (540–604), known to history as Gregory the Great, provides a beautiful model of how to negotiate the difference between colonization and colonialism. Magnanimously, he did not like to be called "pope," "supreme pontiff" or "patriarch of the West," but preferred instead the more homely title: "servant of the servants of God," *servus servorum Dei*. He insisted that a portion of his daily meals be given to the indigent people begging at his door. Oftentimes they would join him at his table. His personal generosity toward the poor, homeless and sick was matched by his global vision of the faith. The world was his mission field. In order to spread the Word and establish the faith in England, he decided to send his trusty librarian, a timid man named Augustine, to carry the standard of Christ north. By the way, *this* Augustine (of Canterbury, as he would one day be known) is a different person than the better known Augustine of Hippo, who died 170 years earlier. Augustine must have wondered what he had done to offend Gregory to be flung from his warm and cozy habitat of books into the wild wilderness of the barbaric Angles. When he arrived, he found little more than an outpost teetering on the edge of civilization. As he tried to make the best of his assignment, Augustine wrote to Gregory and asked his advice on how to negotiate Anglo-Saxon custom, much of which was foreign and backward to his Roman and Christian sensibilities. Gregory responded with grace and dignity,

> the temples of the idols in that nation ought not to be destroyed; but let the idols that are in them be destroyed; let water be consecrated and sprinkled in the said temples, let altars be erected, and relics placed there. For if those temples are well built, it is requisite that they be converted from the worship of devils to the service of the true God; that the nation, seeing that their temples are not destroyed, may remove error from their hearts, and knowing and adoring the true God, may more freely resort to the places to which they have been accustomed.[8]

---

[8]Gregory, in Bede, *Ecclesial History of England,* trans. A. M. Sellar (London: George Bell and Son, 1907), 1.30.

Historian Thomas Cahill interprets this advice as an admonition to "adapt—and love your neighbor as he is, even if he is an Anglo-Saxon."[9]

No need to burn down pagan temples, just replace the pagan images in them with Christian ones. No need to abolish local customs like the Yule log, Easter eggs and wintertime festivals. Instead, find ways to incorporate them into the life of the church. See them as opportunities for discussion, questioning and growth. Instead of banning Halloween activities, host a Trunk-or-Treat or a Fall Festival in the church parking lot. No need for the province of Christ to act provincially; the gospel can absorb all customs and cultures.

The temptation of colonial power assumes many forms—British, American, Chinese, Western, Catholic, Protestant, Muslim, white and masculine. The church must be vigilant against its wooing. "God opposes the proud but gives grace to the humble" (Jas 4:6; 1 Pet 5:5). Christians are commissioned to spread the Word to all people in a loving and respectful manner (1 Tim 2:2). This means honoring people's individuality, heritage and society.

The tension between colonization and colonialism creates crises for the man or woman of God. How should faithful believers fulfill the Great Commission, respect the rights and dignity of others and maintain their distinctively Christian identity? How should Christianity *be* a culture among other cultures? What does a Christian way of life look like in a rapidly evolving twenty-first-century world? Which habits, customs and attitudes should be instilled and insisted on, and which should be dropped?

---

[9]Thomas Cahill, *Pope John XXIII* (New York: Penguin, 2002), p. 20.

15

CHRISTIANITY AS CULTURE

CULTIVATING THE HARVEST

ALASDAIR MACINTYRE (B. 1929), the Scottish born philosopher who has made his career at the University of Notre Dame, once observed,

> It is not the case that men first stopped believing in God and in the authority of the Church, and then subsequently started behaving differently. It seems clear that men first of all lost any overall social agreement as to the right ways to live together, and so ceased to be able to make sense of any claims to moral authority.[1]

What makes people behave differently? What makes people forget time-honored customs of respect and morality? How do communities fall apart? Societies break down when education breaks down. Morality breaks down when discipline and good modeling of the virtues break down. Faith breaks down when discipleship breaks down. The majority of social problems can be traced to a problem with cultivation. The advice of the Proverbs is simple: "Train a child in the way he should go, and when he is old he will not turn from it" (Prov 22:6).

THE CHURCH AT SCHOOL

Cultivation and habituation, encouragement and admonition, training in righteousness and discipleship—these must be the heartbeat and

---

[1]Alasdair MacIntyre, *Secularization and Moral Change* (London: Oxford University Press, 1967), p. 54.

mission of the church today. "The church is always more than a school," says historian Jaroslav Pelikan. "But the church cannot be less than a school. Its faith, hope and love all express themselves in teaching and confession."[2] The best way to combat atheism and secularism is to teach a children's Sunday school class. The old saying is true: every generation of believers is the last. This has nothing to do with the end of the world; it is a statement of fact. No one is born a believer; every generation must be converted, trained and reared. Christian culture cannot be taken for granted. Discipleship, classically known as "catechism," is a perennial task of the pilgrim people of God.

The important church father Gregory of Nyssa (335–394) declared in his *Address on Catechetical Instruction* that "religious catechism is an essential duty of the leaders 'of the mystery of our religion' (1 Tim 3:16). By it the church is enlarged through the addition of those who are saved, while 'the sure word which accords with the [church's] teaching' (Tit 1:9) comes within the hearing of unbelievers."[3] When he visited the city of Jerusalem in 379, he tried to put those words into practice. To his shock and horror, he found the once blessed city of David wracked with corruption and moral decay.

> There is no form of immorality that they do not venture to commit—to say nothing of prostitution, adultery, theft, idolatry, poisoning, envious disputes, murder. . . . Nowhere is murder taken so lightly as it is in those parts. . . . I had promised to confer with the heads of the holy churches in Jerusalem, because their affairs were in confusion and a negotiator was needed.[4]

It is very probable that some of Gregory's negotiations included the handling of catechism, the basic training of new converts and initiates to the faith. If that is true, then it also appears that his reforms had some effect. When Egeria went on pilgrimage to Jerusalem approximately thirty years later, she found a very different city and a very dif-

---

[2]Jaroslav Pelikan, *The Christian Tradition*, vol. 1: *The Emergence of the Catholic Tradition* (Chicago: University of Chicago Press, 1971), p. 1.

[3]Gregory of Nyssa, quoted in Daniel Williams, "Considering Catechism for Suspicious Protestants," *Christian Reflection* 23 (2007): 27.

[4]Gregory of Nyssa *Letter on Pilgrimages* 2.10, NPNF, 2nd series, vol. 5, pp. 42-43.

ferent church than the one Gregory described. She reports with enthusiasm that candidates for baptism and induction into the family of God were required to attend catechesis every day during the eight weeks of Lent leading up to Easter, when they would be baptized. The instructional classes were rigorous, lasting up to three hours a day. The bishop taught them in this way: "beginning with Genesis he goes through the whole of Scripture during these forty days, expounding first its literal meaning and then explaining the spiritual meaning."[5] Egeria proudly exclaims, "In the course of these days everything is taught not only about the Resurrection but concerning the body of faith."[6] Not only were the initiates instructed, they were also examined. Each person must come forward with witnesses and be subjected to a battery of questions: "Does he lead a good life? Does he obey his parents? Is he a drunkard or a liar?"

> If the person proves to be guiltless in all these matters concerning which the bishop has questioned the witnesses who are present, he notes down the man's name with his own hand. If, however, he is accused of anything, the bishop orders him to go out and says: "Let him amend his life, and when he has done so, let him then approach the baptismal font." He makes the same inquiry of both men and women.[7]

As can be seen from the practice at Jerusalem, the process of becoming a Christian can be a long and grueling one. In the same way, planting, weeding, watering and harvesting takes days, weeks and months. Cultivation takes time . . . and cultivation of the heart takes a lifetime. It also takes many hands. Paul tells the Corinthian Christians, "I planted, Apollos watered it, but God made it grow" (1 Cor 3:6). Although the glory and credit always belong to God, each person in the community has an essential role to fill—Paul, Apollos, me, you.

HARVESTING RESULTS

"The harvest is plentiful, but the workers are few. Ask the Lord of the

---

[5]Egeria *Diary of a Pilgrimage* chap. 46, Ancient Christian Writers, vol. 38 (New York: Newman Press, 1970), p. 123.
[6]Ibid.
[7]Ibid., chap. 45.

harvest therefore to send out workers into his harvest" (Mt 9:37-38). Many laborers are needed, for there is much work to do. Although we typically think of the unsaved world as the field of harvest, it is also true that *we*, the church, also need to be plowed, tilled and harvested (Ezek 36:9; 1 Cor 3:9). Cultivation is more than a function of evangelism, it is essential for fruitful Christian life.[8] Indeed, it is a lifelong process of pruning and encouraging, blossoming and reaping (Jn 15:1-6).

Cultivation implies results. As a theological image, it helps frame the process of discipleship, discipline and education in terms of its product. Farmers do not cultivate fields for no purpose; they intend a harvest, a crop, a reward. Well-intentioned church leaders, alas, sometimes plan and conduct Bible studies, vacation Bible school and spiritual retreats as if there were no greater purpose than the activity itself. They can become expected but not exceptional "events" and "opportunities" with little to offer and nothing to demand. But the truth is, education and discipleship do have ends beyond themselves; they are done "in order that you may live a life worthy of the Lord and may please him in every way: bearing fruit in every good work, growing in the knowledge of God" (Col 1:10). And whoever does not bear fruit "is thrown away like a branch and withers" (Jn 15:6). There are expectations and consequences attached with Christian commitment. Like marriage vows, covenant with Christ should not be entered into lightly. "So then, each of us will give account of himself to God" (Rom 14:12). Indeed, there is a final end and aim of Christian cultivation. Socrates proposed that philosophy is preparation for death. Christianity, by contrast, is preparation for *life*—this side of the

---

[8]A rich description of spiritual cultivation is found in Cyril of Jerusalem, who said,

> One and the same rain comes down on all the world, yet it becomes white in the lily, red in the rose, purple in the violets and the hyacinths, different and many-colored in manifold species. Thus it is one in the palm tree and another in the vine, and all in all things, though it is uniform and does not vary in itself. For the rain does not change, coming down now as one thing and now as another, but adapts itself to the thing receiving it and becomes what is suitable to each. Similarly the Holy Spirit, being One and of one nature and indivisible, imparts to each one his grace 'according as he will.' The dry tree when watered brings forth shoots. So too does the soul in sin, once made worthy through repentance of the grace of the Holy Spirit, flower into justice. (*Catechesis* 16.12, Fathers of the Church, vol. 64, p. 82)

Jordan and the other. "If only for this life we have hope in Christ, we are to be pitied more than all men" (1 Cor 15:19).

Let us return for a moment to Gregory of Nyssa. Born third of ten children, he was also the third generation of a notable Christian family in Cappadocia, located now in central Turkey. His two older siblings, sister Macrina and brother Basil, served as important guides and companions for the younger Gregory. Both were major theologians and saints in their own rights. Despite the beneficial familial influence, Gregory did not naturally possess the devotion and drive of Macrina or Basil, nor did he have the education. He was complacent and needed prodding. Visiting the Chapel of the Forty Martyrs, he fell asleep in the arbor. There he dreamed the martyrs came out to beat him with rods. He awoke in a panic, but also full of fervor to follow in his older siblings' footsteps. He joined his brother Basil's monastic community on the family estate in Pontus—a community near the Black Sea for which his brother composed a *Rule*. Basil's *Rule* of organization is still followed by Eastern Orthodox monasteries today. And as for Gregory, he eventually became a major theologian of the church and is still read profitably today.

Gregory, just as much if not more than his siblings, understood and appreciated the fact that cultivation takes time and hard work. It is a lifelong operation, and it does not always, or even often, come naturally. Perfection—the harvest of cultivation—is something we achieve over a lifetime.

> The perfection of everything which can be measured by the senses is marked off by certain definite boundaries. . . . But in the case of virtue we have learned from the Apostle that its one limit of perfection is the fact that it has no limit. For that divine Apostle, great and lofty in understanding, ever running the course of virtue, never ceased *straining toward those* things *that are still to come.* Coming to a stop in the race was not safe for him. Why? Because no Good has a limit in its own nature but is limited by the presence of its opposite, as life is limited by death and light by darkness.[9]

---

[9]Gregory of Nyssa, *Life of Moses*, trans. Abraham Malherbe and Everett Ferguson (New York: Paulist Press, 1978), p. 30, italics his.

During this life we cannot afford to rest in the false security of our achievements and assume we have attained perfection, or nearly enough. "Just as the end of life marks the beginning of death, so stopping the race of virtue marks the beginning of the race of evil."[10] We must, in Solon's phrase, look to the end. If the devil cannot make us atheists, he will make us complacent, which is just as bad, if not worse. For at least the atheist knows she does not believe in God, but the complacent Christian floats along unaware that for all intents and purposes she too is an atheist.

Stopping in the middle of the race is not an option. Paul encourages us to "press on toward the goal to win the prize for which God has called me heavenward in Christ Jesus" (Phil 3:14). Likewise (to change the analogy back to an agricultural one), abandoning the field in the middle of the growing season or the harvest is not an option. "He who gathers crops in summer is a wise son, but he who sleeps during harvest is s disgraceful son" (Prov 10:5). Cultivation and the making of Christian culture present tasks that are never finished. They remain in continual development, enrichment and re-formation (*semper reformanda*—"always reforming"). Nevertheless, in the well-worn hands of the divine farmer and the gentle rain of the Spirit, there will be bountiful harvest.

> For as the soil makes the sprout come up,
> and a garden causes seeds to grow,
> so the Sovereign LORD will make righteousness and praise
> spring up before all nations. (Is 61:11)

---

[10]Ibid.

16

ON BEHALF OF NEW THINGS

"God is dead!" or so at least it seems to us ... until,

round the next bend in the road, "we find him again, alive."

HENRI DE LUBAC

AT TIMES, IT MAY INDEED SEEM that God is dead or perhaps heaving his last breath; we discover, of course, that it is our *idea* of God that has died or been outmoded. God himself is striding far down the path. But he graciously pauses, peers over his shoulder and waves us on.

"From now on I will tell you of new things, of hidden things unknown to you" (Is 48:6). The pattern throughout the Bible is a constant reversal of expectations—when we expect the strong, God chooses the weak; when we expect the firstborn, God chooses the last born; when we expect defeat, God brings victory. The ways of the Lord cannot be guessed or anticipated. The One worshiped by Abraham, Isaac and Jacob is always onto something new, surprising and unforeseen. Our hearts must follow this biblical pattern. Change for the sake of change is not always better. But change for the sake of the gospel and its call is worth making. And the call of the gospel is always a call forward, into the future, into the new.

In 382, the Christian emperor Gratian removed the pagan Altar of Victory from the Senate Hall in Rome. This was the second time the altar had been removed. In 384, after Gratian's death, some members of the senate begged his successor, Emperor Valentinian II, to restore the Altar of Victory as a symbol of Roman pride and power. On behalf of the old stalwarts of the senate, Symmachus requested "that we who are old men may leave to posterity that which we received as boys." Rome herself cries out,

> Let me use my ancestral ceremonies, she says, for I do not repent me of them. Let me live after my own way; for I am free. This was the cult that drove Hannibal from the walls of Rome and the Gauls from the Capitolium. Am I kept for this, to be chastised in my old age?[1]

Opposing the pleas of Symmachus was Ambrose (340–397), himself a former politician and son of a politician. He had given up one form of public service for another: he served the church as the magnetic bishop of Milan. Three years hence this powerful preacher and future saint would baptize Augustine himself into the Christian faith. Ambrose said, with all due respect to Symmachus and the Roman senate,

> Why cite me examples of the ancient? It is no disgrace to pass on to better things. Take the ancient days of chaos when elements were flying about in an unorganized mass. Think how that turmoil settled into the new order of a world and how the world has developed since then, with the gradual invention of the arts and the advances of human history. I suppose that back in the good old times of chaos, the conservative particles objected to the advent of the novel and vulgar sunlight which accompanied the introduction of order. But for all that, the world moved. And we Christians too have grown. Through wrongs, through poverty, through persecution, we have grown.[2]

Ambrose's response reveals an enduring characteristic of the Christian spirit. Christians grow, change and adapt. It is in our DNA. We are compelled to grow. That is part of the nature of faith. We are called to be transformed by the daily renewal of our minds (Rom 12:2). As we grow, so our expressions of faith grow and transform.

There is an ironic footnote to the encounter between Symmachus and Ambrose involving a brilliant young boy named Boethius (c. 475–

---

[1] *Memorial of Symmachus 9*, NPNF, 2nd series, vol. 10, p. 415.
[2] Ambrose *Letter 18*, NPNF, 2nd series, vol. 10, pp. 417-22.

525). The boy was the son of a prominent Roman aristocrat who had died prematurely. Magnanimously, the great-grandson of senator Symmachus, whose full name was Quintus Aurelius Memmius Symmachus, took him into his house and raised him as his own. Memmius Symmachus loved Boethius; Boethius returned the affection and then some by marrying his surrogate father's daughter. The family was happy and harmonious until Boethius was falsely charged with treason, imprisoned in 524 and put to death the next year. Memmius Symmachus was executed by association with his son-in-law in the year following. I raise the name of Boethius not to dwell on the tragedy, but to bring attention to his religious contribution. For, in point of fact, the adopted Boethius adopted the religion of Jesus and became one of the leading Christian philosophers of his day. While awaiting execution he wrote his beloved book on *The Consolation of Philosophy*, a treasury of wisdom. Here he pens words remarkably similar in spirit to those of Ambrose about the ever-pressing obligation to "pass on to better things." Faith demands progress. Trusting that God is not only the source but also the end of all things, Boethius admonishes us,

> If you wish to behold
> The truth in clear light,
> And to take the straight road,
> Forgo empty joys,
> Dismiss every fear,
> Renounce idle hope,
> Let grief come not near.[3]

We must show boldness and exercise courage as we move forward and search deeper. God's reality is higher, lower, wider, deeper and thicker than we can imagine. That is precisely the joy of life in Christ—there is always more. We can know and appreciate the world because God made it good and knowable. And yet precisely because God is the one who made it, it will always be inexhaustible to our minds. We will not master the mysteries of creation nor will we master the mysteries of

---

[3]Boethius, *The Consolation of Philosophy*, trans. W. V. Cooper (Chicago: Regnery Gateway, 1991), p. 11.

Christ. But it is the joy and privilege of Christians everywhere, banded together by our shared quest, to discover and participate in what God is doing in the world.

The case has been made in this book not for new truths, but for new vehicles for the truth. I suggested that Christianity bears many similarities to a story, a language, a game and a culture. Hopefully, these analogies help to fill a need, some lack in our understanding. Hopefully, they communicated truth. But they were never *the* truth. They were vehicles for the truth. Vehicles come and go. As long as they perform their function they have value, but when they cease to perform satisfactorily, they depreciate. Their value depends on their usefulness. Vehicles are meant to be updated, repaired and replaced. [4] It is our duty to search for new vehicles—new ways to express the faith of old. All of our vehicles of comparison and investigation are placed at the service of the people of God as they serve Christ, and as Christ reigns at the service of the Father, with whom he is one, as the people of God strive to be (Jn 17:11). The goal is to do justice to the gospel of Christ in ways that are faithful, loving and hopeful.

One morning in the last year of his life, Francis of Assisi awoke after a night of excruciating and exhausting physical pain. His body was being attacked by multiple ailments that would soon overwhelm him. Even so, he called for one of his companions, a friar, and said that he wished to dictate a new song, a canticle for creation. "I want to write a new *Praise of the Lord* for his creatures, which we use every day, and without which we cannot live."[5] Out of this desire was composed one of the greatest hymns of the Middle Ages, the *Canticle of the Creatures*, Francis's final gift to the world. He understood that the world is ever in need of a new song, a new voice of praise, a new call to worship. May

---

[4]Jerome (347–420) says,

> Put the past out of mind. Set your mind to the future. What he has reckoned perfect today he ascertains to have been false tomorrow as he reaches for ever better and higher goals. By gradual advance, never being static but always in progress, he is able to teach us that what we supposed in our human way to be perfect still remains in some ways imperfect. (*Dialogue Against the Pelagians* 1.14, NPNF, 2nd series, vol. 6, p. 455)

[5]Translated by Donald Spoto, *Reluctant Saint: The Life of Francis of Assisi* (New York: Penguin Compass, 2002), p. 200.

we have courage to follow the Spirit's spontaneity.

> Most High, all-powerful, good Lord:
>> Yours are the praises, the glory
>> And the honor, and all blessing.
> To You alone, Most High, do they belong,
>> And no human is worthy to mention Your name.[6]

---

[6]Ibid.

Name Index

Scripture Index